BOSS UP!
THE OFFICIAL GUIDE TO TEEN ENTREPRENEURSHIP

BY DR. JAMILA T. DAVIS

WITH THE VIP COALITION TEAM

Copyright © 2024 by Dr. Jamila T. Davis with the VIP Coalition Team

All rights reserved. This book or any portion thereof may not be reproduced or used in any manner whatsoever without the express written permission of the publisher, except for the use of brief quotations in a book review.

Product Development: Susan M. Hearn
Creative Director: Triena Smith & Kywuan Warren

Printed in the United States of America

First Printing, 2024
ISBN: 979-8-9903375-4-1

Voices International Publications

INTRODUCTION

Welcome to the thrilling world of entrepreneurship, where dreams ignite, and the possibilities are limitless. I'm Dr. Jamila T. Davis, founder of the VIP School Empowerment Coalition, and I'm here to guide you on this journey toward success.

Through the VIP School Empowerment Coalition, we've vested thousands of teens with the fundamentals of entrepreneurship, equipping them with the knowledge and skills to chase their dreams and build their futures.

But before we go further, let me share my story. I believe sharing my experiences—my wins and losses—will help you understand why I'm so committed to the work I do today.

My journey to entrepreneurship has been one of triumph over adversity, marked by highs and lows but fueled by a relentless determination to make a positive impact. At a young age, I chased success with a hunger for achievement, leading me to become a multimillionaire real estate investor and sought-after celebrity advisor by age twenty-five. However, in 2008 my journey took a detour when I made the wrong choices, resulting in a twelve-and-a-half-year sentence in federal prison for bank fraud.

Let's go back and explore where I first went off course. In 1991, as a teen attending Fiorello LaGuardia High School of Performing Arts in Manhattan, New York, I yearned for freedom and sought validation in all the wrong places. Like many of you, I wanted to be one of the "cool kids." In those days, being cool often meant having a boyfriend.

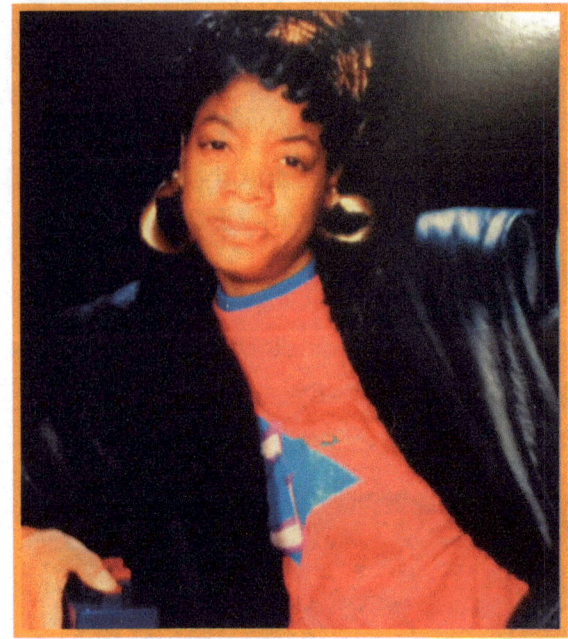

During my first week of school, I met my first boyfriend, and he seemed to embody everything I thought I wanted—popularity, status, and access to money. However, there was a dark side to his allure; he was a drug dealer from the 40 Projects, which is a housing project in South Jamaica, Queens, New York.

Despite knowing the risks, I found myself drawn to him, blinded by the illusion of his lifestyle. His money and status brought me a sense of notoriety and belonging that I craved as a young girl. But as quickly as our relationship began, it came crashing down when he dumped me for a sixteen-year-old girl who made her own money as a baker.

The pain of heartbreak was unbearable, and it was my first encounter with trauma that I never truly healed from. Not knowing how to deal with my emotions, I turned to the pursuit of money as a means of validation and empowerment, embarking on a journey that ultimately led to self-destruction and hardship.

During my time in prison, I refused to let my circumstances define me. Instead, I seized the opportunity to transform my life. I pursued education relentlessly, earning several degrees, including my associate's, bachelor's, and master's degrees.

From behind bars, I even began coursework for my Ph.D. In addition to my academic pursuits, I discovered a passion for writing and authored over a dozen books, including the Voices of Consequences Enrichment Series, specifically tailored to empower incarcerated women. Today, this series is an approved curriculum by the Bureau of Prisons, where women receive time off their sentences for completion.

I realized that my purpose extended far beyond the confines of prison walls; I had a gift and a mission to inspire and empower others. Making a promise to God, I vowed to use my experiences to guide others away from my mistakes and towards a path of success from the inside out.

Upon release, I hit the ground running, determined to turn my pain into purpose. Returning to the very place where my journey took a detour, I went back to high school, but this time as an educator and mentor. Through the VIP School Empowerment Coalition, I dedicated myself to empowering teens, sharing my experiences and insights to help guide them toward a brighter future. Drawing from my journey, I used my findings to complete my dissertation and earned my Ph.D.

So, from being federal prisoner #59253-053, I transformed into Dr. Jamila T. Davis. My story captured the attention of major network shows such as BET's American Gangster, ABC's Pink Collar Crimes, and VH1's True Crime Story, shedding light on my journey and the invaluable lessons I've learned along the way. I use my story as a cautionary tale, a reminder to others of the consequences of poor choices and the transformative power of redemption.

As a serial entrepreneur, I've experienced the pitfalls of pursuing success the wrong way and the triumphs of doing it the right way. Since coming home from prison, I've founded several successful businesses, including Black Women's Lives Matter, a media platform providing resources and support to Black women and girls. Today, this platform has over 325,000 followers, empowering countless individuals with knowledge and community.

To support this work, I created Pink Passion Apparel, a clothing line that uplifts and inspires Black women. Starting with just $500, we've generated over a million dollars in sales, proving that with determination and passion, anything is possible.

Today, I'm not only an entrepreneur but a social entrepreneur. I create businesses that give back to my community, making a meaningful difference in the lives of others. This book is a part of my mission to inspire young people like you and teach you the power you hold within. My goal is to help you succeed without making the mistakes I once did. This manual is written with love and care. It will be the roadmap many of you use to gain financial freedom. If you follow the steps, you are arming yourself with powerful information that can break generational curses and help you, too, to be successful!

So now that you know who I am, my mission, and my purpose, let's journey together as we explore the transformative power of entrepreneurship and the boundless opportunities it can create for you and so many others through you. The best part is that you don't have to wait until you grow up to be a high-level achiever. Together, we can make it happen now! Just like myself, you were born to be a changemaker. It's time for action!

Dr. Jamila T. Davis

BOSS UP!
THE OFFICIAL GUIDE TO TEEN ENTREPRENEURSHIP

TABLE OF CONTENTS

CHAPTER 1: IF YOU CAN SEE IT, YOU CAN BE IT!
Discover inspiring stories of young Black entrepreneurs and learn how to develop the mindset needed to turn passion into business success.

CHAPTER 2: MONEY TALKS: MASTERING FINANCIAL LITERACY
Learn how to earn, save, and invest wisely, master budgeting basics, and navigate the world of credit and debt with confidence.

CHAPTER 3: PLAN, PREPARE & CONQUER: FROM PASSION TO PROFIT
Discover how to find your passion, identify market opportunities, research your idea's viability, and turn it into a solid business plan for success.

CHAPTER 4: CRAFTING YOUR BRAND: STAND OUT AND SHINE
Learn how to create a brand that reflects who you are, develop a unique value proposition, and use social media to amplify your presence.

CHAPTER 5: PRODUCT SOURCING AND BUDGETING
Explore strategies for finding quality products at affordable prices, master budgeting essentials for growth, and learn negotiation techniques for cost-effective purchases.

CHAPTER 6: MARKETING MASTERY: CULTIVATING YOUR COMMUNITY
Understand your target audience, craft compelling marketing strategies, and dive into digital marketing with tips and tricks to boost your business.

CHAPTER 7: CONTENT CREATION
Learn to create engaging content across platforms, master visual storytelling with images and videos, and build a loyal following through consistency and authenticity.

CHAPTER 8: ESTABLISHING YOUR PRESENCE ON THE INTERNET
Discover how to create a professional website, leverage social media for brand visibility, and engage your audience with compelling content.

CHAPTER 9: CUSTOMER SERVICE AND BUSINESS ETIQUETTE
Learn strategies for customer satisfaction, navigate professional communication across various settings, and resolve customer issues with grace and efficiency.

CHAPTER 10: PRODUCING YOUR POP-UP SHOP
Learn the essentials of planning, organizing, and executing a successful pop-up shop, from selecting the perfect location to creating an unforgettable customer experience.

APPENDIX: BUSINESS MANAGEMENT CASE STUDIES
Explore case studies that highlight leadership, teamwork, and collaboration.

ARE YOU READY TO BOSS UP?

CHAPTER 1
IF YOU CAN SEE IT, YOU CAN BE IT!

Introduction to the Exciting World of Entrepreneurship

There are many misconceptions about entrepreneurship, or "being a boss," and owning your own business. Yes, it offers freedom and other benefits, but it also demands a new way of thinking and a unique set of skills to be successful.

Entrepreneurship is more than just starting a business; it requires embracing a mindset that empowers you to create your own path and seize opportunities where others see challenges.

In this chapter, we'll explore the exciting world of entrepreneurship, dispel common myths, and uncover the keys to success in today's dynamic business landscape. Are you ready to embark on this transformative journey?

Let's dive in!

1 IF YOU CAN SEE IT, YOU CAN BE IT!

In our community, entrepreneurship has always been a beacon of hope, a way to overcome obstacles and build a better future. Throughout history, Black entrepreneurs have been trailblazers, carving out their own paths and inspiring others to do the same.

From Madam C.J. Walker, who built a haircare empire from scratch to Oprah Winfrey, who turned her passion for media into a global empire, the stories of Black entrepreneurs are a testament to the power of resilience and determination.

But entrepreneurship isn't just for the history books; it's a tool any of us can use to create a better life for ourselves and our communities. That's why we're here today: to introduce you to the exciting possibilities of entrepreneurship and help you cultivate the mindset and skills you need to succeed.

Through the Boss Up Teen Entrepreneurship Program, we teach that entrepreneurship is more than just a business; it's a way of life. Our program is designed to empower young people like you to take control of your futures and create opportunities for yourself, no matter where you come from or what challenges you may face.

> In this book and in our course, you'll learn everything you need to know to become a successful entrepreneur.
>
> From developing a business idea to creating a marketing plan and managing your finances, we'll cover all the essentials you'll need to launch and grow your business.

But more than that, you'll learn how to think like an entrepreneur—to see opportunities where others see obstacles, to take risks, and to persevere in the face of adversity. Ultimately, success in entrepreneurship isn't just about what you know; it's about who you are and how you approach the world.

Trey Brown featured on ABC 7 NY

I believe in the rule of law: "In order to be it, you must first see it." There are many examples of successful teen entrepreneurs all across our country, each with their own unique stories of resilience and determination. Let me introduce you to a few standout individuals making waves in the entrepreneurial world.

One remarkable teen entrepreneur is Trey Brown, the founder and CEO of SPERGO®, a trendsetting streetwear and lifestyle brand based in Philadelphia, Pennsylvania. Trey's journey began with a simple yet powerful vision to make a positive impact on his community.

Back in 2018, Trey reached out to me via DM, seeking support to promote his brand. His story instantly resonated with me. Trey's entrepreneurial journey started at the age of twelve when he became increasingly aware of the violence plaguing his community. Determined to make a difference, he used his leftover birthday money to purchase sixteen t-shirts, which he sold out in just one week.

Recognizing the potential to combine his passion for design with his desire to inspire youth, Trey officially launched SPERGO on Martin Luther King Day in 2018. His message of courage and strength quickly gained traction, reaching over 20,000 people in the first year alone.

In just thirty-six months, Trey has achieved remarkable success, selling over 30,000 units of merchandise and grossing more than $200,000 in sales for several consecutive months. His brand has garnered attention from national celebrities and media outlets, including Meek Mill, Tierra Whack, and Da Baby.

Zandra Cunningham, Founder, Zandra Beauty

Beyond entrepreneurship, Trey is also a sought-after youth speaker, sharing his story and empowering others at schools, community events, and youth shelters. He has been featured in advertising campaigns, received recognition from local officials, and even received a key to the city of Philadelphia for his community work

Despite his achievements, Trey remains grounded and committed to giving back to his community. In his free time, he contributes to back-to-school drives, visits sick children, feeds the less fortunate, and serves in his hometown church.

As Trey looks to the future, his plans include expanding SPERGO internationally, growing his team, opening flagship stores, and mentoring other young entrepreneurs. With his unwavering determination and commitment to making a difference, Trey Brown is just getting started on his journey to success. He is no different than many of you. He simply dared to dream and acted on it!

Another remarkable individual stands out in our journey of discovery into the world of young entrepreneurs: Zandra Cunningham. Zandra's entrepreneurial journey began at nine in humble beginnings in Buffalo, New York. Her desire to find the perfect lip balm sparked her curiosity and set her on the path to creating her natural skincare products.

Zandra embarked on a mission to develop products that were effective and made with natural ingredients. She started experimenting with formulations in her kitchen, driven by her passion for skincare and determination to make a difference.

What sets Zandra Beauty apart is its core philosophy: a dedication to using natural ingredients that are beneficial for the skin and the environment. Zandra firmly believes in the power of natural substances, and this belief is reflected in every aspect of her business, from product formulation to packaging.

Grand Opening of 17 Year Old, Ryan Kundan's Restaurant

Throughout her journey, Zandra has learned invaluable lessons that she eagerly shares with aspiring entrepreneurs. She emphasizes the importance of persistence, passion, and resilience in the face of challenges. Zandra's story serves as a testament to the fact that age is no barrier to success; with dedication and perseverance, anything is possible.

Despite her young age, Zandra's company has achieved remarkable success. Zandra Beauty has generated millions of dollars in revenue thanks to Zandra's vision and determination. As Zandra Beauty continues to thrive and grow, Zandra remains focused on the future, constantly seeking new opportunities for innovation and expansion.

Zandra Cunningham's journey is a shining example of what can be achieved through passion, determination, and a commitment to excellence. With courage and perseverance, we can turn our dreams into reality.

Now that you've been inspired by the stories of Trey and Zandra, it's time to envision yourself walking alongside them as a successful teen entrepreneur.

Let's gain some more knowledge so you can decide what business works best for you.

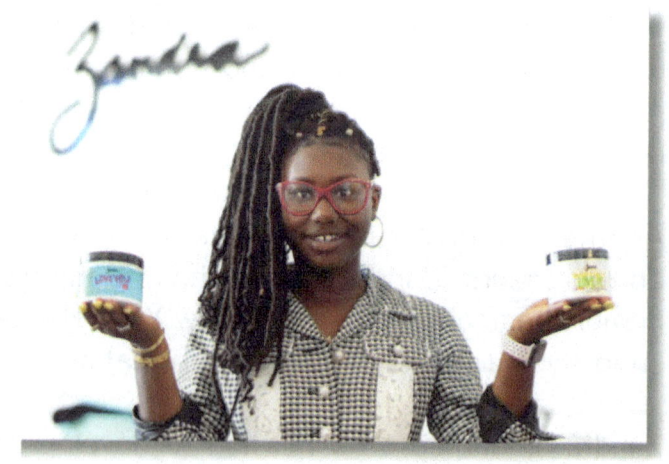

Zandra Cunningham, featured with her products in Because of Them We Can

PRODUCT-BASED VS. SERVICE-BASED BUSINESSES

In our exploration of entrepreneurship, it's crucial to understand the difference between service- and product-based businesses. A service-based business focuses on providing intangible services to clients, such as consulting, coaching, or freelance work.

In contrast, a product-based business involves selling tangible goods, like clothing, accessories, or handmade crafts. Each type of business comes with its own challenges and opportunities, so choosing the model that aligns best with your skills, interests, and resources is essential.

> **1. Product-Based Business:**
> Imagine you have a lemonade stand. You make delicious lemonade and sell it to people who pass by. In a product-based business, you're selling something tangible, like a physical item or product. So, in this case, the lemonade you make and sell is the product. You might focus on making different flavors, creating eye-catching signs, or finding the best location to attract customers.
>
> **2. Service-Based Business:**
> Now, let's say you offer to walk dogs in your neighborhood. People who are busy or at work might need someone to take their furry friends for a walk during the day. In a service-based business, you're offering your time and skills to help others. So, in this case, the service you provide is walking dogs. You might advertise your services by posting flyers on social media or around the neighborhood, talking to pet owners, or creating a profile on a pet-sitting website.

In simple terms, a product-based business sells things you can touch or hold, like lemonade or handmade crafts, while a service-based business offers help or assistance to others, like dog walking or tutoring. Both types of businesses can be successful, depending on what you enjoy and are good at.

So, whether you're making something to sell or offering your time to help others, there are plenty of opportunities to start your own business and make a difference in your community.

Remember, the key to success in any business venture is to offer value to your customers and provide excellent service. So, choose a business idea that aligns with your interests and skills and addresses your target audience's needs. With creativity, determination, and a willingness to learn, you have the power to turn your entrepreneurial dreams into reality, just like Trey and Zandra.

IDEAS FOR TEEN BUSINESSES

You might be wondering, "How can I start my own business?" The good news is that you have lots of options. First, take some time to think about your passions, interests, and the problems you wish to solve for others. By identifying what resonates with you, you can uncover potential business ideas that align with your interests and skills. Below are some examples of businesses that teens can start with $500 or less:

1. Customized Clothing or Accessories: Design and sell personalized t-shirts, hats, jewelry, or other accessories tailored to your target audience's preferences.

2. Handmade Crafts: Create and sell handmade crafts such as candles, soaps, artwork, or knitted items through online platforms or local markets.

3. Digital Services: Offer digital services such as graphic design or social media management as well as editing services to YouTubers, small businesses, or individuals looking to enhance their video content. You can charge a monthly fee for your services and potentially manage multiple clients simultaneously, making it a flexible and lucrative business.

4. Pet Services: Provide pet-sitting, dog-walking, grooming, or training services in your neighborhood.

5. Home Services: Offer lawn care, gardening, house cleaning, or organizing services to busy families or individuals in your community.

6. Baked Goods: Bake and sell homemade cookies, cupcakes, or specialty treats at local events, farmers' markets, or online.

7. Tutoring or Coaching: Offer tutoring services in subjects you're passionate about or provide coaching in areas such as sports, music, or fitness.

8. Reselling: Purchase discounted items from thrift stores, garage sales, or online marketplaces and resell them at a higher price for profit.

9. Hair Braiding, Weaving, or Wig Making: If you have skills in hairstyling, consider offering hair braiding, weaving, or wig-making services.

10. Video Editing: Offer your editing services to YouTubers, small businesses, or individuals looking to enhance their video content.

11. Babysitting or Childcare: Offering babysitting or childcare services for a few hours after school or on weekends can provide a steady income while helping busy parents.

GOAL SETTING

Now, let's talk about goal setting, a fundamental aspect of entrepreneurship, guiding you on your journey to success. Setting clear, achievable goals provides direction, motivation, and a roadmap for your entrepreneurial endeavors. Whether short-term or long-term, goals help you stay focused, measure progress, and celebrate achievements along the way.

Short-term goals are those that you aim to accomplish within a relatively short period, typically within a few weeks to a year. These goals are essential for maintaining momentum and staying on track toward your larger objectives. They could include launching a website, acquiring your first paying customer, or completing a certification course relevant to your business.

On the other hand, **long-term goals** are the big-picture objectives you strive to achieve over an extended period, often spanning several years or even a lifetime. These goals provide a sense of purpose and vision, guiding your decisions and actions as you work towards your ultimate aspirations. Examples of long-term goals might include reaching a particular revenue milestone, expanding into new markets, or becoming a recognized leader in your industry.

By setting both short-term and long-term goals, you create a roadmap for success, breaking down your larger vision into manageable steps and milestones. Remember, goal setting is not just about what you want to achieve; it's also about who you want to become in the process. So, dream big, set ambitious goals, and let your entrepreneurial journey unfold with purpose and determination.

Now, are you ready to dream big and start young? Are you ready to take control of your future and build the life you've always dreamed of? If so, then let's embark on this journey together.

The world is waiting for you to make your mark, and with the right mindset and skills, there's no limit to what you can achieve.

Let's get started!

GROWTH WORK
DEFINE YOUR ENTREPRENEURIAL VISION

Take some time to reflect on your entrepreneurial aspirations and define your vision for success. Ask yourself the following questions:

What does entrepreneurship mean to you personally, and how can it impact your life and community?

Can you name some successful entrepreneurs you admire? What qualities or values do they possess that inspire you?

What products or services do these entrepreneurs offer, and how do their actions or business practices positively impact their community or industry?

GROWTH WORK
LET'S DIG A LITTLE DEEPER

Do you believe you have what it takes to become a successful entrepreneur? Why or why not? Reflect on your strengths and areas for growth.

What products or services do you envision selling to generate income? How do these ideas align with your interests, skills, and passions?

What are some of your business goals for the next few years? How do these goals align with your personal growth and long-term aspirations?

BOSS UP | CHAPTER 1 | PAGE 17

GROWTH WORK
NOW DREAM BIG!

How much revenue do you aim to generate through your business in the next five years?

SHORT-TERM REVENUE GOALS

90 Days: $ _____   Year 1: $ _____

6 Months: $ _____

LONG-TERM REVENUE GOALS

Year 2: $ _____   Year 4: $ _____

Year 3: $ _____   Year 5: $ _____

Setting a clear revenue goal for the next five years is like plotting your destination on a map—it gives you direction and purpose. Aim high and let your ambition drive you to innovate, hustle, and grow.

Remember, every milestone you achieve along the way brings you closer to transforming your business dreams into reality. Believe in your potential and let your goals inspire you to reach new heights!

GROWTH WORK
SEE YOURSELF IN OTHERS

 Research successful teen entrepreneurs online. Identify one you admire, describe their business, and highlight a few characteristics they possess. How can you apply these traits to your own entrepreneurial goals and values?

GROWTH WORK
CRAFTING YOUR VISION BOARD

Financial literacy is a powerful tool that can empower individuals to take control of their financial destinies. By learning how to save, understanding the ins and outs of banking, and distinguishing between assets and liabilities, you can embark on a journey toward financial freedom and generational wealth. Remember, knowledge is power, and anything is possible with the right knowledge.

This chapter laid the foundation for understanding entrepreneurship by emphasizing the importance of vision and self-belief. Now, it's time to turn those ideas into concrete actions. Let's dive into the Growth Work and start mapping out your own entrepreneurial journey.

Imagine yourself as the successful individual you're destined to become. In the real-world exercise, we'll plan and budget as if we're living in the real world. Start by identifying your career path, projected income, preferred living situation, transportation, and estimated living expenses. Once these key aspects are outlined, we'll create a realistic budget to determine if your desired lifestyle is financially feasible.

Now, let's take the next step in visualization...

  USE QR CODE FOR ACCESS TO YOUR CANVA ASSIGNMENTS

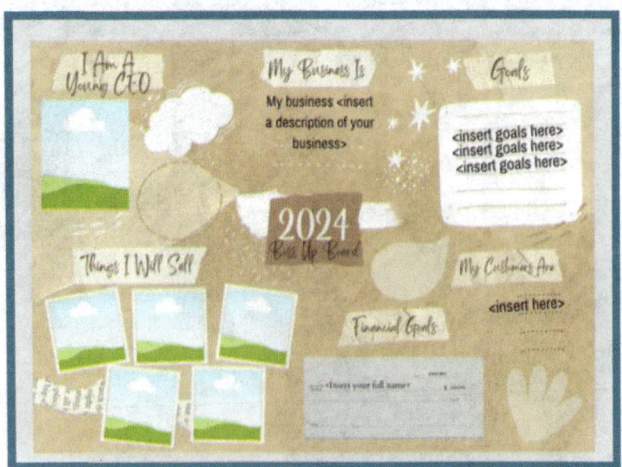

Before

After

Example of Vision Board Template in Canva

GROWTH WORK
CRAFTING YOUR VISION BOARD

Let's craft a Canva vision board that captures your financial aspirations and business goals. This exercise will guide you in visualizing and planning your journey toward success.

Self Image

Begin by uploading a selfie or a photo of yourself, symbolizing your role as a young CEO. This represents your identity and commitment to your business.

Business Description

My Business Is

My business <insert a description of your business>

Use Canva's text tool to briefly describe your business and the products or services you offer. This should give a clear overview of what your business is all about.

Business Goals

<insert goals here>
<insert goals here>
<insert goals here>

Identify and list at least three goals you have for your business. These can be related to growth, revenue, product development, or any other aspect important to you.

Products or Services

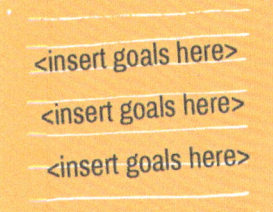

Add images representing the products or services you plan to provide. Use Canva's elements or upload your own images to visually depict what you offer.

Target Audience

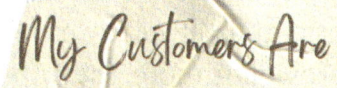

<insert here>
<insert here>
<insert here>

Identify and list at least three key target audiences for your business, considering demographics, interests, and challenges they face

Financial Goals

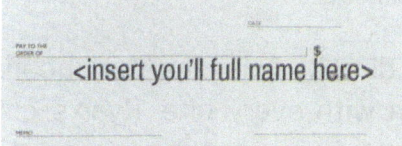

<insert you'll full name here>

Visualize your financial success by writing a "check" to yourself.

Indicate the amount you aim to earn from your business and the date you plan to achieve this goal.

EXCERPT FROM TEEN MAGAZINE SUMMER 2024 EDITION

From Passion to Profit: Boss Up Teen Entrepreneur Ryan's Journey with Everything Nice with Spice

By Zaniyah Austin

At just 17 years old, Ryan Kundan is defying the odds and turning his passion for Caribbean cuisine into a thriving business venture. It brings him joy to speak about his business and passion. Alongside his mother, he has created Everything Nice with Spice, a groundbreaking restaurant that brings the vibrant flavors of Guyanese, Jamaican, and Trinidadian food to their community in East Orange. This restaurant may very well be the first of its kind in the area, making it a significant milestone for the local community.

Ryan's journey began during the COVID-19 pandemic, with funding from his mother and a shared love for cooking. Together, they infuse every dish with love and tradition, creating a culinary experience that goes beyond just satisfying hunger. Their business, which started as a catering venture, quickly gained popularity for its authentic flavors and heartfelt service.

What sets Everything Nice with Spice apart is their commitment to inclusivity. While honoring their Caribbean roots, they offer not only hearty meals but also vegan options and refreshing smoothies, ensuring there's something for everyone to enjoy. "We want everyone to feel welcomed and valued," Ryan says. This inclusive approach has endeared them to a diverse customer base and reinforced their reputation as a community-centric business.

Inspired by his mother, who hails from Georgetown, Guyana, Ryan aims to create an atmosphere where stepping into their restaurant feels like stepping into the Caribbean itself. "It's not just about the money for us," Ryan explains. "We want each customer to feel the warmth and hospitality of the Caribbean." This commitment to customer experience extends beyond their restaurant doors—they regularly extend their generosity to the homeless, providing more food than what's paid for.

Ryan and Family pictured at Grand Opening

Importing spices directly from the Caribbean, Everything Nice with Spice aims to evoke a sense of vacation with every bite. Ryan's culinary skills, passed down from his mom and grandmothers, not only ensure the success of their restaurant but also lay the foundation for his mom's additional venture—setting up cruise planners for those dreaming of traveling to the Caribbean.

**EXCERPT FROM TEEN MAGAZINE
SUMMER 2024 EDITION**

Equipped with training from the Boss Up entrepreneurship course and support from his mother, Ryan officially opened Everything Nice with Spice in his hometown on June 15, 2024!

Everything Nice with Spice isn't just a business; it's a labor of love that's bringing a taste of the Caribbean to the world, one dish at a time. The anticipation was high as they prepared for the grand opening of the restaurant in East Orange on June 15, 2024. This special event featured a ribbon-cutting ceremony with community members and Mayor Ted Green, marking a significant milestone in Ryan's entrepreneurial journey.

Ryan Kundan's story is a testament to the power of passion and perseverance. At such a young age, he is already making a significant impact, not only by sharing his love for Caribbean cuisine but also by enriching his community.

BOSS UP | CHAPTER 1 | PAGE 23

CHAPTER 2
MONEY TALKS:
MASTERING FINANCIAL LITERACY

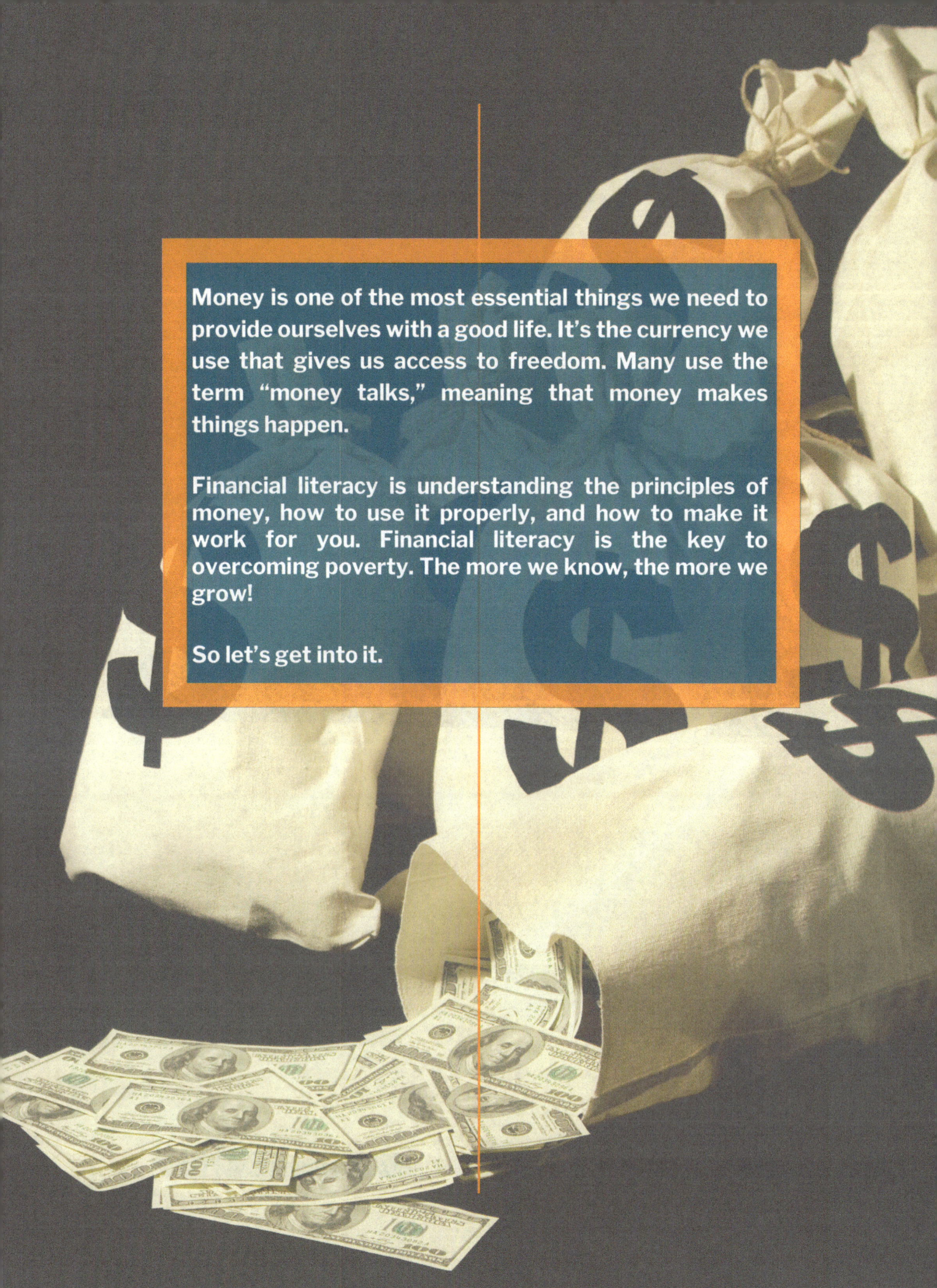

Money is one of the most essential things we need to provide ourselves with a good life. It's the currency we use that gives us access to freedom. Many use the term "money talks," meaning that money makes things happen.

Financial literacy is understanding the principles of money, how to use it properly, and how to make it work for you. Financial literacy is the key to overcoming poverty. The more we know, the more we grow!

So let's get into it.

2 MONEY TALKS

Poverty is a big problem, especially in communities where people of color live. Poverty means not having enough money or resources to live comfortably, putting families in tough financial situations. Systemic barriers and unfair treatment rooted as far back as slavery make it even harder for residents to thrive.

This cycle of struggle can get deeply rooted, passing on poverty from one generation to the next and making it hard to move forward personally and as a community. When resources are scarce, people might feel like they have to take risks or do illegal things to make money, making it even harder to break free from poverty. This not only affects individuals and families but also takes away opportunities and hope from our community, holding us back and keeping inequality alive.

Understanding how to manage money and make smart financial decisions is crucial in breaking the cycle of poverty in communities of color. Financial literacy empowers individuals to take control of their finances, build wealth, and secure a stable future for themselves and their families. By learning about budgeting, saving, investing, and avoiding debt traps, people can make informed choices that lead to economic stability and growth. With financial knowledge, we can break free from the grips of poverty, create opportunities for ourselves, and work towards a brighter and more prosperous future.

Growing up, I witnessed firsthand the transformative power of financial literacy. Let me take you on a journey to Queens, New York, where I was born and raised by two incredibly hard-working parents. But my story began long before I was born. It starts in a small town called Kinston, nestled in the heart of North Carolina. This is where my parents embarked on a journey that would change our family's trajectory forever.

You see, my parents knew the harsh realities of poverty all too well. They grew up with very little but refused to let their circumstances define their future. Armed with determination and a thirst for knowledge, they pursued education, which became their ticket to escape poverty. My mother went to college, and my dad went to the U.S. Army and then attended vocational school.

In the 1960s, they boldly decided to move north, seeking better opportunities and a chance to break free from the chains of financial hardship. My mother became a school teacher, and my dad became a New York City Transit supervisor. They saved their money, and when they had enough for a down payment, they took a leap of faith and purchased their first home in Queens, New York, for $30,000. Little did they know that this investment would become the cornerstone of our family's wealth for generations. Fast forward to today, and that same home is worth well over $600,000 — and it's completely paid off.

It didn't stop there. My father, in particular, understood the power of investing wisely. He seized opportunities in real estate, acquiring multi-family homes and renting them out to tenants. The rent money these tenants paid was used to pay his mortgages, and he had cash left over to save and invest more. Over time, these properties provided a steady income stream and appreciated in value, turning my father into a multimillionaire. Watching this, I knew I wanted to have my share of the American dream.

But here's the thing: success isn't just about making money—it is about using it wisely. My father wasn't handed a silver spoon; he had to carve out his own path to success. And now, he's passing down a legacy of wealth to his children, a legacy built on the foundation of financial literacy.

You see, the difference between the rich and the poor isn't about how much money you have—it's about access to information and opportunities. Owning a home is one of the easiest ways to build generational wealth. Many people who rent can actually afford to own their homes instead, but they lack the knowledge and guidance to make it happen. That's where financial literacy comes in.

Financial literacy is the cornerstone of building wealth and achieving financial freedom. It encompasses a range of skills and knowledge, from understanding basic budgeting to navigating complex investment strategies. By mastering these principles, individuals can take control of their financial futures and create lasting legacies for themselves and their families.

Knowledge is power, and my mission is to empower you with the tools and insights you need to confidently navigate the world of finance. So, let's start with the basics:

Teen entrepreneur proudly standing in front of his vendor table

Savings

We will begin by discussing the importance of saving. Saving money isn't just about stashing away cash for a rainy day. Effective saving involves cultivating a mindset of financial responsibility and preparedness. Whether that means setting aside a portion of your allowance or paycheck, saving regularly is a crucial habit that lays the foundation for future financial success. Let's break it down:

When people save money, they usually put it in a bank. But what exactly is a bank, and why do we trust them with our hard-earned cash? Think of a bank as a safe place to keep your money. It's like a big, secure vault where you can deposit your savings and withdraw them whenever you need. But banks do more than just hold onto your money—they also offer services like checking and savings accounts, loans, and investment opportunities.

You might wonder why we put our money in a bank instead of under our mattress. Well, there are a few reasons:

1. Safety: Banks are heavily regulated and insured, so your money is protected against theft, loss, or other risks. Plus, they have security measures in place to keep your funds safe.

2. Convenience: Imagine carrying around all your savings in cash—it would be bulky and risky. Banks offer convenient ways to access your money, like debit cards, online banking, and ATMs, so you can manage your finances wherever you are.

3. Interest: When you deposit money in a savings account, the bank pays you interest. This is like a little bonus they give you for keeping your money with them. Over time, your savings can grow thanks to compound interest, earning you even more money.

So, in simple terms, a bank is like a trustworthy friend that helps you keep your money safe and accessible and even helps it grow over time. It's a vital part of the financial system that empowers individuals like you to manage your finances wisely and achieve your goals.

Navigating Credit and Debt

When you create a relationship with a bank, you're not just opening a savings account—you're also setting yourself up to have access to credit. But what exactly is credit, and why is it important?

Credit is a financial tool that allows you to borrow money or buy things now and pay for them later. It's like getting an extra boost when you need it, whether for buying a car, paying for college, or even starting a business.

You might be wondering why credit matters. Well, here are a few reasons:

1. Building a Good Reputation: When you borrow money and pay it back on time, you show that you're responsible and trustworthy. This builds your credit history, which is like your financial report card. A good credit history can open doors for you, such as getting approved for loans or renting an apartment.

2. Access to Opportunities: Access to credit means you can take advantage of opportunities that come your way, whether buying a house or investing in your education. Instead of waiting years to save enough money, credit allows you to seize these opportunities now and reap the rewards later.

3. Growing Wealth: Now, here's where it gets really interesting. When used wisely, credit can help you acquire wealth. For example, taking out a loan to start a business can lead to higher earnings and financial independence. Using a credit card to build your credit history can qualify you for lower interest rates on future loans, saving you money in the long run.

So, credit can help you build a solid financial foundation and create opportunities for yourself. By understanding how to use credit wisely and responsibly, you can leverage it to acquire wealth and achieve your dreams. It's just one more piece of the puzzle on your journey to financial success.

The Budgeting Basics

Now that you understand the importance of savings and credit, let's discuss budgeting. Budgeting helps us to:

1. Manage Our Money: Budgeting is like giving every dollar a job to do. It helps us keep track of how much money we have coming in and going out to ensure we're not spending more than we earn. This is important for staying on top of our finances and avoiding debt.

2. Reach Our Goals: Whether saving up for a new phone, going on vacation, or buying a car, budgeting helps us prioritize our spending to reach our goals faster. By setting aside money for specific purposes, we can make sure we're making progress toward what's important to us.

3. Prepare for the Unexpected: Life is full of surprises, both good and bad. Budgeting helps us prepare for the unexpected by setting aside money for emergencies or unexpected expenses. This way, we're not caught off guard when things don't go as planned.

Student Omya Foreman discussing business plans

So, why is budgeting important? Here are a few reasons:

1. Financial Control: Budgeting puts us in the driver's seat of our finances. Instead of wondering where our money went at the end of the month, we know exactly where it's going and why. This gives us a sense of control and peace of mind.

2. Reduced Stress: Money problems can be a significant source of stress and anxiety. Budgeting can alleviate some of that stress by ensuring we're managing our money responsibly and working towards our goals.

3. Long-Term Financial Success: Budgeting isn't just about managing our money in the short term—we're also setting ourselves up for long-term financial success. By developing good budgeting habits early on, we can build a solid financial foundation that will serve us well for years to come.

How do we budget? It's actually pretty simple:

1. Track Your Income: Start by figuring out how much money you have coming in each month, whether it's from a job, allowance, or other sources.

2. List Your Expenses: Next, make a list of all your expenses, from rent and groceries to entertainment and savings goals. Be sure to include everything, no matter how small.

3. Allocate Your Money: Now, divide your income among your expenses, making sure to prioritize your needs and goals. This might mean cutting back on non-essential spending or finding ways to increase your income.

4. Stick to Your Budget: Once you've created your budget, stick to it! Track your spending throughout the month and make adjustments as needed to stay on target.

Remember, budgeting is a powerful tool that can help us take control of our finances and achieve our goals. By making it a habit and staying disciplined, we can set ourselves up for a lifetime of financial success.

My dad taught me a valuable lesson: It's not just about how much money you make but what you do with it. Budgeting plays a crucial role in this process by helping us see our money clearly and plan what we will do with it. Many people fall into the trap of wasting their money on material things, only to find themselves with nothing to show for it in the end.

That's where understanding the difference between **assets and liabilities** comes in. So, what exactly are assets and liabilities, and why are they important?

- **Assets** are things that put money in your pocket or increase in value over time. This could include investments, real estate, or even a business that generates income. Essentially, assets help you build wealth and create financial security for the future.

- **Liabilities** drain your financial resources and can hold you back from achieving your financial goals.

The importance of understanding the difference between assets and liabilities cannot be overstated. By acquiring assets and minimizing liabilities, you can build wealth and create a solid financial foundation for yourself and your family.

So, the next time you're tempted to splurge on something that won't bring you long-term value, remember the wise words of my dad: It's not just about how much money you make, but rather what you do with it. Focus on building assets, and you'll be well on your way to financial success.

GROWTH WORK
MONEY TALKS DISCUSSION

Let's review what was covered in this chapter. How do the concepts and lessons apply to your life and goals?

What are the benefits of having money, both personally and for the community?

What is financial literacy, and why is it important for personal and community well-being?

What is poverty, and how does it affect individuals and communities?

GROWTH WORK
MONEY TALKS DISCUSSION

What is generational wealth, and how can it benefit you and your community?

```
┌─────────────────────────────────────────────────────────────┐
│                                                             │
│                                                             │
│                                                             │
│                                                             │
└─────────────────────────────────────────────────────────────┘
```

How did Dr. Davis's family build generational wealth, and what lessons can we learn?

```
┌─────────────────────────────────────────────────────────────┐
│                                                             │
│                                                             │
│                                                             │
│                                                             │
└─────────────────────────────────────────────────────────────┘
```

What are the benefits of keeping your money in a bank, and how can it help you achieve your financial goals?

```
┌─────────────────────────────────────────────────────────────┐
│                                                             │
│                                                             │
│                                                             │
│                                                             │
└─────────────────────────────────────────────────────────────┘
```

GROWTH WORK
MONEY TALKS DISCUSSION

What two major accounts can you open at a bank, and how can they help you manage your money responsibly?

What is credit, and how can understanding credit and debt responsibly help you achieve your financial goals?

What are assets? Name one and explain its importance for building wealth.

GROWTH WORK
MONEY TALKS DISCUSSION

What are liabilities? Name one and discuss its impact on financial health.

How can budgeting help you manage money better and achieve your goals?

After these exercises, how do you feel about your financial knowledge and personal progress?

GROWTH WORK
VISUALIZE YOUR MONEY TALKING

After completing these exercises, transfer this information to Canva to build your vision board visually representing your financial aspirations and goals.

What is your dream job title or career aspiration? Write it down, reflecting on how it aligns with your passions and goals.

How much do you aspire to earn annually with your career success? Write down your target income based on your goals.

$ _____ per year

What is your expected monthly income? Calculate this by dividing your annual income goal by 12.

$ _____ per month

PRO TIP

Want to know how much you could earn in your dream job? Check out websites like Indeed.com. They have easy-to-understand salary information based on where you want to live, what you want to do, and how much experience you have.

GROWTH WORK
VISUALIZE YOUR MONEY TALKING

Describe your dream house's size, style, and details. How do you envision feeling when waking up in it or coming home after a long day?

Describe the ideal neighborhood and state for you. Consider the community vibe, available amenities, lifestyle, and how living there will impact your daily happiness and well-being.

Will you rent or own your home?

What will your monthly rent or mortgage be? Calculate this by dividing your annual housing cost by 12.

$ _____ per month

PRO TIP

Looking to get an idea of housing costs in your dream neighborhood? Zillow.com is a great resource! You can search for rentals or homes for sale in specific areas, explore property details, and even estimate monthly mortgage payments.

GROWTH WORK
VISUALIZE YOUR MONEY TALKING

 What kind of car do you envision driving? Describe its make, model, features, and how driving it will make you feel in terms of comfort, excitement, and pride.

What is the cost of your dream car? Research and note the price.

$

What will your monthly payments be for your dream car?

$

per month

PRO TIP

Looking for your dream car? Check out Cars.com! You can search for cars based on make, model, year, and price range, making it easy to find options that fit your budget.

GROWTH WORK
VISUALIZE YOUR MONEY TALKING

Evaluate whether your dream occupation can support your desired lifestyle by covering monthly expenses. If necessary, consider adjusting these goals to better align with the lifestyle you envision for yourself.

Income vs Expenses

I want to make $ _____

minus 25% taxes = $ _____

(÷ annual by 12) this will give me $ _____

I will save (20%) of my monthly salary $ _____

Monthly Expenses

Rent/Mortgage $ _____

Car Note $ _____

Self Care $ _____

Fun $ _____

Utilities $ _____

Insurance $ _____

+Monthly Savings $ _____

The actual monthly salary I need is: $ _____

GROWTH WORK
YOUR SMART MONEY VISION BOARD

Let's craft a Canva vision board that captures your financial aspirations and business goals. Map out your dreams and the steps to reach them. Then, we'll translate this into your vision board, creating a visual reminder of your money-smart journey.

Begin by uploading a selfie or a photo of yourself, symbolizing your role as a young CEO. This represents your identity and commitment to your business.

Use the text tool to list your career goals. Whether you aspire to be an entrepreneur, a lawyer, or another professional, specify your desired career path and the financial goals associated with it.

INCOME VS EXPENSES

I WANT TO MAKE	$	/YEAR
− 25% TAXES =	$	/YEAR
(ANNUAL BY 12) THIS WILL GIVE ME	$	/MONTH
I WILL SAVE (20%) OF MY MONTHLY SALARY	$	

Use the text tool to list your career goals. Whether you aspire to be an entrepreneur, a lawyer, or another professional, specify your desired career path and the financial goals associated with it.

USE QR CODE FOR ACCESS TO YOUR CANVA ASSIGNMENTS

Calculate your estimated monthly expenses based on your lifestyle choices. Include costs for housing, transportation, self-care, and entertainment. Use tools like calculators or online resources to get accurate estimates.

**EXCERPT FROM TEEN MAGAZINE
SUMMER 2024 EDITION**

Meet Vincent: The Fearless Teen Fashion Designer of 4Klaws

By Mia Mack

Vincent Trevino, at 16 years old, is the creative force behind 4Klaws, a fashion brand that's determined to take the industry by storm. Founded in 2022, 4Klaws specializes in designing, manufacturing, and selling unique apparel that reflects Vincent's fearlessness and individuality.

From the outset, Vincent's vision for 4Klaws was clear: to create streetwear that stands out and makes a statement. His debut collection of shirts sold out completely, thanks to his one-of-a-kind designs and attention to detail and quality. With 20 shirts priced at $20 each, Vincent's commitment to affordable yet premium apparel shines through.

What sets 4Klaws apart is Vincent's dedication to his craft. He values the quality of his apparel and takes immense pride in his work. Drawing inspiration from brands like Hellstar and his father's personal style, Vincent says, "I would only see my dad dress that way, making it a unique style for me."

Initially starting with shirts, 4Klaws has now expanded its range to include hoodies, beanies, sweatpants, and jeans, catering to both girls and guys who appreciate a unique sense of style. "Because of the popularity of my first drop, I want to have better-quality clothes." Vincent's marketing strategy, centered around Instagram and TikTok, has garnered him a loyal following and attention from fashion enthusiasts.

But for Vincent, 4Klaws is more than just a business; it's a reflection of his emotions and personal connection to his designs. Each piece is infused with an emotion he believes will resonate with his customers, allowing them to connect with the brand on a deeper level.

Despite his young age, Vincent is investing all of his revenue back into 4Klaws, ensuring that the brand maintains its outstanding quality and continues to push boundaries in the fashion industry. Through his passion, creativity, and unwavering dedication, Vincent is proving that age is no barrier to success in the world of fashion. Keep an eye on 4Klaws—this is just the beginning of Vincent's journey to fashion greatness.

CHAPTER 3

PLAN, PREPARE & CONQUER:
FROM PASSION TO PROFIT

Now, it's time to secure the bag with no holes. We are going to do that by creating our own business. In this chapter, we'll equip you with the tools and strategies you need to plan, prepare, and conquer the world of business, all while staying true to your unique passions and interests.

Isaiah Stewart, 16-Year-Old Owner of Urban Kids Filit, A Financial Literacy Business for Youth

3 PLAN, PREPARE & CONQUER: FROM PASSION TO PROFIT

Business Structures

As a teen entrepreneur, it's important to understand the different business structures available to you. The most common options are below:

Sole Proprietorship

This is the simplest and most common form of business ownership. As a sole proprietor, you are the only owner of your business and are personally responsible for its debts and liabilities. This structure is ideal for small, low-risk businesses operated by individuals.

For example, a teenager starts a small baking business from home. The teen is the sole proprietor of the business, handling all aspects of baking, marketing, selling, and managing the business independently. They are personally responsible for the company's success and liabilities.

In most states, sole proprietors are not required to register their businesses at the state level. However, there are exceptions, and it's essential to check the specific requirements of the state where the business operates. This can generally be done by a simple Google search.

Typically, sole proprietors need to register their business if they operate under a name other than their own legal name. This is often called a "Doing Business As" (DBA) or trade name. Registering a DBA ensures that the business name is officially recognized and can be used for banking, contracts, and other business transactions.

Additionally, certain professions or industries may require licensing or permits, which may involve registration at the state level. Sole proprietors must research and comply with all applicable regulations and requirements to operate their businesses legally and avoid potential penalties.

> **In a sole proprietorship, Sarah is the sole owner of the cupcake business. She bakes the cupcakes, sets the prices, and handles all aspects of the business on her own. Sarah is personally responsible for any debts or issues that may arise.**

Partnership

If you're starting a business with one or more partners, a partnership may be the right structure for you. In a partnership, two or more people share ownership of the business. They are jointly responsible for its debts and liabilities. Partnerships can be general partnerships, where all partners have equal responsibility and liability, or limited partnerships, where some partners have limited liability.

For example, two teenage friends decide to start a tutoring service together. They form a partnership where they both contribute their skills and resources to the business. They share the responsibilities of teaching, marketing, and managing the tutoring service, as well as the profits and risks associated with the business.

In most states, partnerships are not required to register their business at the state level. However, similar to sole proprietorships, partnerships may need to register if they operate under a name other than the legal names of the partners. This is typically known as a "Doing Business As" (DBA) or trade name registration.

Additionally, partnerships may need to obtain certain licenses or permits depending on the nature of their business and the industry in which they operate. These requirements can vary by state and locality, so it's essential for partnerships to research and comply with all relevant regulations.

> **In a partnership, Sarah and her friend Lisa start a cupcake business together called Sweet Duo Cupcakes. They share responsibilities, with Sarah handling baking and Lisa managing marketing and sales. Both partners contribute to the business and share profits, but they are also personally responsible for any debts or legal issues that arise.**

Corporation

A corporation is a separate legal entity owned by shareholders. Unlike sole proprietorships and partnerships, corporations provide limited liability protection to their owners, meaning shareholders are not personally responsible for the company's debts and liabilities. Corporations are more complex to set up and operate than other business structures and are subject to more stringent regulatory requirements.

In essence, a corporation acts as its own person. It is issued an Employee Identification Number (EIN number), which is similar to a person's social security number.

Here is an example of how a sole proprietorship and a corporation differ:
Imagine a teenager named Sarah who loves baking and decides to start selling her cupcakes to her classmates.

Corporation (cont.)

> In a corporation, Sarah and her friends form a company called "Sweet Treats, Inc." Each friend becomes a shareholder in the corporation, and they collectively make decisions about the business. The corporation is a separate legal entity from the owners, providing limited liability protection for the shareholders.

To set up a corporation as a teen entrepreneur, you can follow these simplified steps:

- **Step 1. Choose a Name**: Pick a unique name for your corporation that follows the rules in your state.

- **Step 2. Fill Out Paperwork:** Fill out and submit the required forms called Articles of Incorporation to create your corporation officially. This form is generally filed with your state's Secretary of State. For a fee, legal services online, such as Legal Zoom, will assist with this filing.

- **Step 3. Create Rules:** Write down the rules for how your corporation will be run (bylaws) and choose people to be in charge (directors and officers).

- **Step 4. Hold a Meeting:** Meet to finalize the rules, choose leaders, and get everything set up.

- **Step 5. Get Permits and Licenses:** Ensure you have any permits or licenses needed to run your business legally.

- **Step 6. Share Ownership:** If other people are joining your business, issue them ownership shares (stock).

- **Step 7. Keep Records:** Keep good records of important documents and decisions, and make sure to follow the rules for running a corporation.

PRO TIP

Getting help from adults or professionals when setting up a corporation is a good idea to ensure you do everything correctly.

Limited Liability Company (LLC)

An LLC combines the limited liability protection of a corporation with the flexibility and tax benefits of a partnership. In an LLC, owners are not personally liable for the company's debts and liabilities, and profits and losses are passed through to the owners' personal tax returns.

For example, a teenager named Alex wants to start a small graphic design business. Alex decides to form an LLC for the business, where they are the sole member. This structure provides Alex with limited liability protection while allowing them to operate the business independently.

The main difference between an LLC and a corporation is the level of formality and structure. Here are some key differences:

- **Formation:** Forming an LLC is generally more straightforward and requires less paperwork than forming a corporation.
- **Management:** LLCs have more flexibility in management structure and decision-making than corporations, which have a more rigid structure with a board of directors and officers.
- **Taxation:** LLCs have pass-through taxation, meaning profits and losses flow through to the members' personal tax returns. Corporations may face double taxation, where the corporation is taxed on its profits and shareholders are taxed on dividends.
- **Liability:** Both LLCs and corporations provide limited liability protection, but the specific rules and requirements may vary based on state laws and the type of business.

Overall, an LLC is a popular choice for small businesses and startups due to its flexibility, simplicity, and limited liability protection for the owners.

When choosing a business structure, consider factors such as liability protection, taxation, and administrative requirements. Consult with a legal or financial advisor to determine the best structure for your specific circumstances.

Teen Entrepreneur students discussing business details

Limited Liability Company (LLC) (cont.)

Operational Considerations

Once you've chosen a business structure, it's time to think about how you'll operate your business on a day-to-day basis. Consider the following operational considerations.

- **Business Location:** Will you operate your business from home, rent a commercial space, or operate online? Consider factors such as cost, convenience, and access to your target market.
- **Financial Management**: How will you handle finances, including budgeting, bookkeeping, and taxes? Consider using accounting software or hiring a professional accountant to help you manage your finances.
- **Product or Service Delivery:** How will you deliver your products or services to customers? Will you offer delivery, shipping, or in-person pickup options? Consider logistics such as packaging, shipping costs, and delivery times.
- **Customer Service:** How will you provide customer support and address inquiries or complaints? Consider implementing systems such as email support, live chat, or a dedicated customer service phone line.
- **Legal and Regulatory Complianc**e: What legal and regulatory requirements apply to your business? Consider factors such as business licenses, permits, zoning regulations, and industry-specific regulations.

By carefully considering these operational considerations, you can ensure that your business runs smoothly and efficiently, setting the stage for long-term success.

Teen Entreprenuers sharing their baked goods and products with potential new customers at Juneteenth Pop Up Shop in Brooklyn, New York

RESEARCHING YOUR IDEA: IS IT VIABLE?

Finding Your Passion and Identifying Market Opportunities

Now that you understand business structure, let's explore your passions. Your passions are more than just interests; they're the driving force behind your entrepreneurial journey. Think of them as superpowers that give your business its unique edge. Whether you're drawn to gaming, fashion, music, or social justice, these passions are the core of your identity and what makes your venture special. To uncover what truly excites you, ask yourself:

- What activities make me lose track of time?
- When do I feel most alive and energized?
- What causes or topics am I deeply passionate about?

This authentic alignment with your passions is what will fuel your creativity, perseverance, and overall success.

Aligning Passion with Market Demand

Passion alone won't secure your success. To thrive, you need to bridge your interests with market opportunities. Dive into various industries and explore where your passions align with current market needs. Understand the desires and challenges of your target audience:

- Who are they?
- What problems do they face?
- How can your unique offerings address these needs?

Whatever your idea may be, take the time to explore different industries and markets to identify areas where your passion aligns with market demand. This is where the magic happens—where your unique talents and interests meet the needs of your audience, creating a winning formula for success.

Now that you've explored how your passions can fuel your entrepreneurial journey and align with market opportunities, you're ready to start turning those ideas into action. By combining what you love with what people need, you're setting yourself up for success.

Keep your enthusiasm high and stay curious about how your interests can meet real-world demands. With this foundation, you're all set to move forward and start building something amazing.

TEEN-FRIENDLY BUDGET-FRIENDLY BUSINESSES

Starting a business as a teen doesn't have to break the bank. With a budget of $500 or less, there are plenty of opportunities to turn your passions into profitable ventures. Here are some ideas to consider:

Customized Clothing: If you're passionate about creating, turn your craft into a business. For example, Jamal, known for his fashion sense, decides to start an online store selling printed T-shirts. He channels his passion for fashioned creativity into a successful online venture, offering unique, personalized items to customers.

Tutoring Services: If you excel in a particular subject, there's always a need for tutoring. Ava, who has a knack for math, recognizes that many middle school students struggle with algebra. By offering tutoring services, she aligns her strengths in math with the needs of students seeking academic help.

Lawn Care or Pet Sitting: If you enjoy working outdoors or caring for animals, these services are in demand. Emily, who loves spending time outdoors, sees a need for reliable lawn care in her neighborhood. By offering to mow lawns and water plants, she meets the needs of busy families while doing what she enjoys.

Social Media Management: If you're savvy with social media, many small businesses need help managing their accounts and creating engaging content. For example, David, who excels at crafting compelling posts, offers his services to local businesses aiming to enhance their online presence and connect with their audience.

Online Reselling: If you're passionate about vintage fashion, turn that interest into a business. For example, Sophia loves finding unique clothing and accessories at thrift stores. She combines her passion for vintage finds with a profitable venture by reselling these items online through platforms like Depop and eBay.

Hair Braiding, Weaving, or Wig Making: If you're passionate about hairstyling, you can turn your love for braiding into a business. For example, Rose enjoys creating intricate braid styles and stylish custom wigs and sees a growing demand for services. She started offering personalized services in her neighborhood.

CREATING YOUR BUSINESS PLAN

Bringing Your Business Idea to Life
Once you've chosen a business idea, the next step is to think about how you'll make it a reality. This means considering how you'll run your business day-to-day and how you'll reach potential customers. Before diving into the specifics, take a moment to envision what your business will look like and how it will operate

Operating Your Business
Think about who will assist you in running your business—whether it's family, friends, or other entrepreneurs. Plan the logistics: where you'll sell your products or services, how you'll manage finances, and how you'll handle orders or appointments. These operational details are essential for keeping your business running smoothly and efficiently.

Marketing Your Business

Marketing is key to attracting customers and growing your business. You'll explore effective marketing strategies in more detail in an upcoming chapter, but start thinking about how to leverage social media platforms like Instagram, TikTok, and Facebook to showcase your products. Encourage satisfied customers to spread the word to help build your brand.

Preparation for Your Business Plan
Creating a business plan isn't just a step—it's a transformative journey that guides you to success. It's your personal blueprint, lighting the way and helping you grow in several key ways.

A business plan turns your dreams into clear, actionable goals, giving you direction and purpose. It sets milestones and timelines, helping you stay motivated and track progress. A business plan evolves with you, fostering flexibility and resilience. It details costs, pricing, revenue, and profit for informed decisions. It guides you on gathering and analyzing market trends. Your plan ensures you're aware of necessary permits and licenses. Incorporating feedback helps you improve products and services.

We've created an easy-to-use template to help you get started. Let's embark on this journey together and build your business plan!

CREATING A MISSION STATEMENT, VISION STATEMENT, AND EXECUTIVE SUMMARY

To start your business plan, think of the mission statement as your compass, guiding you with your business's purpose and values. The vision statement is like a lighthouse, illuminating your long-term goals and dreams and helping you navigate through challenges. Meanwhile, the executive summary serves as your map, offering a clear overview of where you're headed, what you'll encounter, and how you plan to reach your goals. Let's dive in and craft each of these components together.

Mission Statement

To craft your mission statement, consider your business's core purpose and the impact you aim to have on your customers and community. Reflect on the values and principles that guide your business decisions. For instance, Sarah's mission statement for her Etsy shop could be: "To spread warmth and joy through handcrafted knitwear while promoting sustainability and creativity." This statement encapsulates her business's purpose and the positive influence she hopes to have.

Vision Statement

Your vision statement should express your long-term goals and aspirations for your business, capturing the future impact you envision. For example, Ava's vision statement for her tutoring services might be: "To empower students to achieve academic success and unlock their full potential, one lesson at a time." This statement outlines Ava's ultimate goal and the positive change she hopes to bring through her business.

Executive Summary

Your executive summary is a short overview of your business plan. It includes key points like your business concept, target market, competitive analysis, marketing strategy, and financial projections. Start by writing a draft to help organize your thoughts. After completing the full business plan, finalize the executive summary to ensure it includes all the most important information. Keep it clear and concise so anyone reading it understands your business idea and its potential.

These key elements—your mission statement, vision statement, and executive summary—help you clearly define your business's purpose, direction, and goals. As you work on these parts, keep them simple, inspiring, and true to your values. This strong foundation will help your business grow and stay focused on reaching your goals.

CREATING REALISTIC BUSINESS GOALS

Setting realistic business goals is crucial for measuring progress and staying focused. By defining clear and actionable objectives, you create a roadmap for your success. Begin by using the **S.M.A.R.T**. criteria to define your goals:

- **Specific:** Clearly define what you want to achieve. A specific goal has a much greater chance of being accomplished than a general one. For example, instead of saying "increase sales," specify "increase monthly sales by 20%."

- **Measurable:** Establish criteria for measuring progress. This could be metrics like sales numbers, customer satisfaction ratings, or social media engagement. Being able to measure your progress keeps you motivated and on track.

- **Achievable**: Set challenging yet attainable goals. Consider your resources, skills, and time available. For example, if you're just starting out, aiming to become a top seller in a niche market might be more realistic than competing with established giants.

- **Relevant:** Ensure your goals align with your broader business objectives and values. The goal should make sense within the context of your overall business strategy and help you move forward in the right direction.

- **Time-bound:** Set a deadline for your goals. This creates a sense of urgency and helps you prioritize your tasks. For instance, aim to achieve a specific milestone within six months.

For example, Sophia's SMART goal for her online reselling business might be: "To increase monthly sales by 20% within the next six months by expanding inventory and improving product photography." This goal is specific, measurable, achievable, relevant, and time-bound, providing a clear target to strive for.

Once you've set your SMART goals, break them down into smaller, actionable steps and create a timeline for achieving them. Regularly review and adjust your goals based on your progress and changing circumstances.

By starting with a clear vision, setting realistic SMART goals, and staying focused on your mission, you'll be well on your way to building a successful business as a teen entrepreneur.

Remember, entrepreneurship is a journey—embrace the challenges, celebrate the victories, and always strive for greatness.

GROWTH WORK
ENTREPRENEURSHIP ROADMAP: FROM PASSION TO PROFIT

By answering these questions, you're not just scribbling down ideas – each step brings you closer to realizing your dreams.

What kind of business do you plan to create? Describe the industry, products, or services offered and your vision for its impact and success.

What is the name of your business? Explain what it means and why you chose it.

Who is your target audience? Describe the people who will benefit most from your product or service.

GROWTH WORK
ENTREPRENEURSHIP ROADMAP: FROM PASSION TO PROFIT

What business structure will you choose? Explain whether it will be a sole proprietorship, partnership, LLC, or corporation and why.

How does your passion make you feel, and why is it important to you? Can you see this passion becoming a business that excites and motivates you every day?

How can your passion address the needs or challenges of others? Consider the potential audience and market demand. Do you believe there is a viable business opportunity here, and why?

GROWTH WORK
YOUR S.M.A.R.T. GOALS

What are 3-5 SPECIFIC business goals you want to achieve?

1.

2.

3.

4.

5.

GROWTH WORK
YOUR S.M.A.R.T. GOALS

How will you MEASURE your progress towards these goals?

Are these goals ACHIEVABLE given your current resources and skills?

How are these goals RELEVANT to your personal and business aspirations?

What is your time-bound deadline for achieving these goals?

GROWTH WORK
STARTING YOUR BUSINESS PLAN

Create Your Mission Statement

Your business's mission statement is its heartbeat—it explains why your business exists and what it aims to do for customers. Here's how to start:

Identify a specific issue or need that your business addresses. This could be a gap in the market, a common challenge customers face, or a way to improve their lives.

Think about your long-term goals, the positive impact you want to have, and how you envision your business contributing to your community, industry, generation, or beyond.

Describe the specific benefits your products or services offer to your customers. Think about how you can make their lives easier, better, or more enjoyable, and what sets your offerings apart from others.

GROWTH WORK
STARTING YOUR BUSINESS PLAN

Create Your Vision Statement

Your business's vision statement is its guiding star—it outlines your long-term aspirations and the impact you aim to have on the world. Here's how to start:

Think about the long-term changes or improvements you want to make in your community or industry. What difference do you want to see, and how will your business lead the way?

Describe your aspirations for your business's growth and success. What milestones do you want to reach, such as expanding your services, gaining a loyal customer base, or becoming a well-known name in your city and beyond?

Reflect on the legacy you want your business to leave. How do you want to be remembered, and what lasting contributions do you want to make? Think about the values and principles that will define your business's legacy.

GROWTH WORK

STARTING YOUR BUSINESS PLAN

Create Your Executive Summary

Your executive summary is a snapshot of your business plan, giving a quick overview of the most important aspects. Here's how to craft it:

Start by providing a quick description of your business. Mention the products or services you offer.

[ ]

Explain who your customers are. Who are the people that will buy your products or use your services?

[ ]

Talk about what sets your business apart from others. Why should customers choose you over the competition?

[ ]

GROWTH WORK

STARTING YOUR BUSINESS PLAN

Continue Creating Your Executive Summary

Briefly describe how you plan to reach your customers. This could include social media, advertising, or other methods.

Give an overview of your financial plans, like how much money you hope to make and any funding you need.

End with your main goals for the business. What do you hope to achieve in the future?

GROWTH WORK
RESEARCH

Research and analyze the business strategies of a company you admire or that is similar to yours.

This assignment encourages you to analyze real-world examples of successful companies and draw insights to assist your entrepreneurial endeavors.

Which company have you chosen to analyze, and why does it inspire you?

What is the company's mission statement, and how does it align with its overall business strategy?

What is the company's target market, and how does it cater to their needs?

What products or services does the company offer?

GROWTH WORK

RESEARCH

 **What marketing strategies does the company use to promote its products or services?**

```
┌──────────────────────────────────────────────────────────┐
│                                                          │
│                                                          │
│                                                          │
└──────────────────────────────────────────────────────────┘
```

Reflecting on the company's strategies, what aspects do you find most interesting or inspiring?

```
┌──────────────────────────────────────────────────────────┐
│                                                          │
│                                                          │
│                                                          │
└──────────────────────────────────────────────────────────┘
```

How could you apply elements of the company's strategies to your entrepreneurial aspirations or business ideas?

```
┌──────────────────────────────────────────────────────────┐
│                                                          │
│                                                          │
│                                                          │
└──────────────────────────────────────────────────────────┘
```

SAMPLE CANVA BUSINESS PLAN TEMPLATE

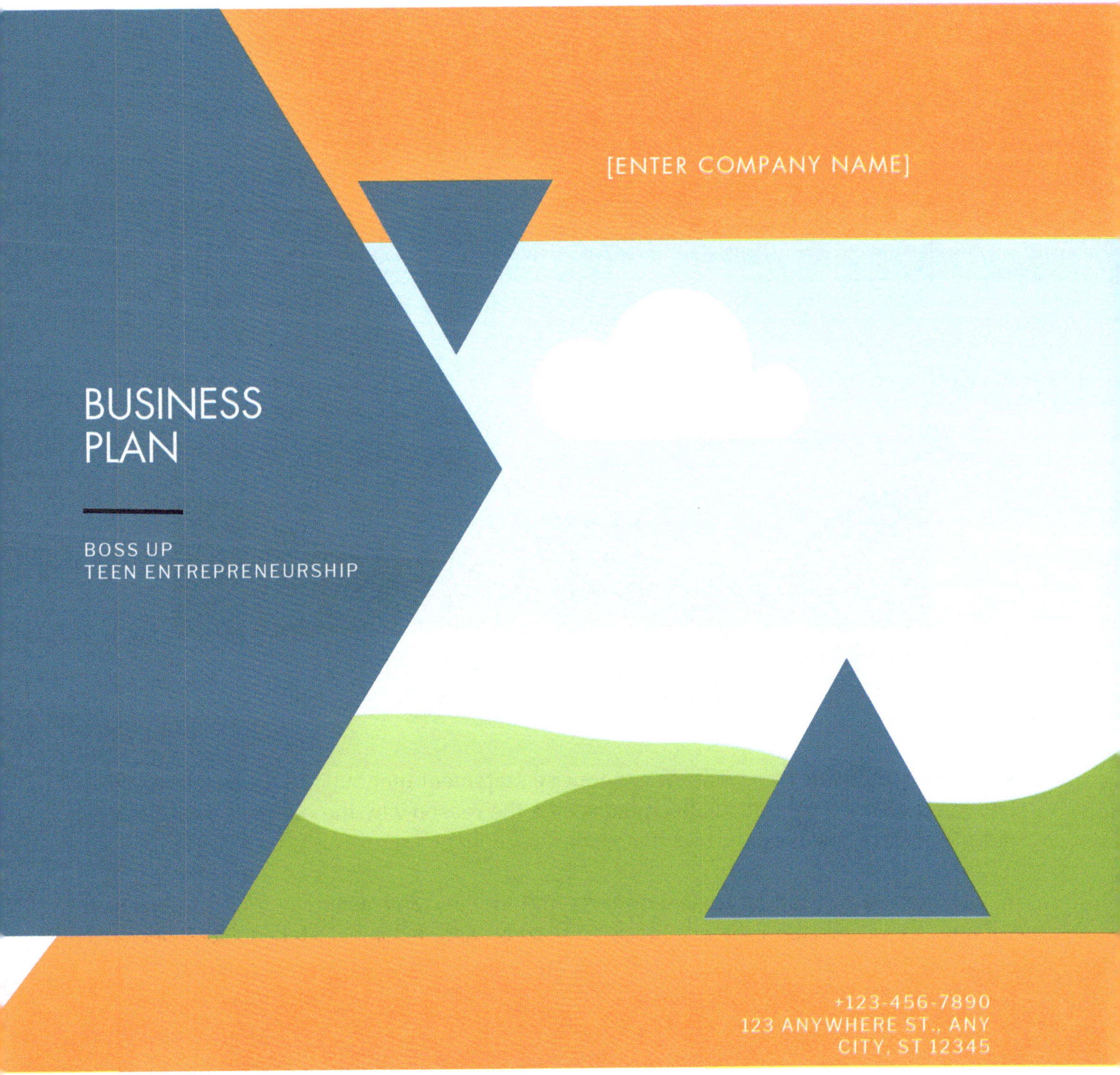

[ENTER COMPANY NAME]

BUSINESS PLAN

BOSS UP
TEEN ENTREPRENEURSHIP

+123-456-7890
123 ANYWHERE ST., ANY CITY, ST 12345

USE QR CODE FOR ACCESS TO YOUR CANVA ASSIGNMENTS

SAMPLE CANVA BUSINESS PLAN TEMPLATE

ABOUT COMPANY

MISSION STATEMENT

A mission statement for a business is a concise statement that outlines the purpose, values, and goals of the organization. It communicates the reason why the business exists, what it aims to achieve, and the principles that guide its actions.

A well-crafted mission statement reflects the identity and aspirations of the business, serving as a guiding light for decision-making and inspiring stakeholders, including employees, customers, and investors.

SAMPLE CANVA BUSINESS PLAN TEMPLATE

PROJECT & BACKGROUND
VISION STATEMENT

VISION STATEMENT

A vision statement for a business is a forward-looking statement that articulates the long-term aspirations and goals of the organization. It describes the desired future state or outcome that the business aims to achieve, providing a clear picture of what success looks like.

A vision statement is often ambitious, inspiring, and aspirational, capturing the organization's dreams for the future. It serves as a guiding beacon, motivating and aligning stakeholders towards a common purpose and direction.

SAMPLE CANVA BUSINESS PLAN TEMPLATE

BUSINESS GOALS

TOP BUSINESS GOALS
[DESCRIBE YOUR TOP BUSINESS GOALS]

▶ **GOAL #1**

▶ **GOAL #2**

▶ **GOAL #3**

▶ **GOAL #4**

▶ **GOAL #5**

SAMPLE CANVA BUSINESS PLAN TEMPLATE

EXECUTIVE SUMMARY

An executive summary of a business plan is a brief overview of the key points contained within the full business plan document. It typically includes essential information such as the business concept, target market, unique selling proposition, financial highlights, and growth projections.

The executive summary provides readers with a snapshot of the business opportunity, highlighting its potential for success and the key strategies for achieving business goals. It serves as an introduction to the business plan, enticing readers to delve deeper into the details of the document.

A well-crafted executive summary should be concise, engaging, and persuasive, capturing the attention of investors, partners, or stakeholders and compelling them to explore the business plan further.

SAMPLE CANVA BUSINESS PLAN TEMPLATE

NEW BUSINESS BUDGET PROPOSAL

#	Startup Expenses	Category	Amount
1	Ex. Beads (100 count)	Supplies	$29.99
		TOTAL	$

EXCERPT FROM TEEN MAGAZINE SUMMER 2024 EDITION

Meet ZewdeiNesh Gowdie: The Vegan Entrepreneur Making Waves with RastaGirl Loyal's Vegan Treats

ZewdeiNesh and Councilman Christopher Awe

Introducing ZewdeiNesh Gowdie, an 18-year-old culinary genius and entrepreneur extraordinaire. As the head of RastaGirl Loyal's Vegan Treats, ZewdeiNesh is revolutionizing the world of vegan cuisine, one delectable treat at a time.

Born into a Jamaican and Trinidadian heritage, ZewdeiNesh's passion for cooking and baking runs deep. Raised in America, she brings a wealth of cultural knowledge to her culinary creations, infusing them with the rich flavors and traditions of her upbringing.

ZewdeiNesh, her mother and Director Dr. Jamila T. Davis

ZewdeiNesh's journey into entrepreneurship began during her sophomore year of high school when she started baking homemade treats for her peers. Word quickly spread about her mouthwatering brownies, cookies, ziti, and more, and soon, RastaGirl Loyal's Vegan Treats was born. "It started off with just my friends, then got popular with others around the school."

ZewdeiNesh differentiates herself with her commitment to veganism. As a lifelong vegan, she not only understands the health and environmental benefits of a plant-based lifestyle but also aims to make veganism more accessible and appealing to others. "I usually don't tell people that the treats are vegan, I just let it speak for itself." With her delectable creations, she hopes to show people that vegan food can be just as delicious and satisfying as its non-vegan counterparts.

In addition to her thriving business, ZewdeiNesh is a multi-talented individual. She is a self-made rapper who writes her own tracks, using her platform to spread messages of empowerment and positivity. With plans to collaborate with others in the future, ZewdeiNesh is poised to make waves in the music industry as well.

But her talents don't stop there. ZewdeiNesh also excels in hairstyling, specializing in locs and other unique styles. Despite her many endeavors, she manages her business single-handedly, with unwavering support from her family, who assist with cooking and cleaning.

Looking ahead, ZewdeiNesh dreams of opening her own shop after graduation, where she can continue sharing her passion for veganism and culinary creations with the world.

The social justice issue of veganism is important to her. She speaks about the social, economic, and environmental impact of veganism. With her determination, talent, and entrepreneurial spirit, there's no doubt that ZewdeiNesh Gowdie is destined for greatness.

Keep an eye out for RastaGirl Loyal's Vegan Treats, a taste sensation you won't want to miss!

What is Brand Strategy?

FINDING BRAND MAGIC

Hey there, future moguls!

This chapter is written by your girl Tiffany Williams, aka Ms. Bellargo, the creative force behind one of the largest streetwear brands in Philly: **Bellargo Piarge**. Today, I want to share with you the eight-letter word that turned my $500 hustle into a seven-figure empire over the past 20 years: branding. And that's where branding comes into play!

Boss Up Entrepreneur Instructor, Tiffany Williams, CEO & Founder of Bellargo Piarge Street Wear

4 CRAFTING YOUR BRAND: STAND OUT AND SHINE!

I cannot stress enough how many entrepreneurs I've seen overlook the central role of branding in their business endeavors. In entrepreneurship, many ventures falter not due to a lack of passion or creativity but a lack of understanding and connection with the audience. Whether you're dreaming big or starting small, realizing your customers' pivotal role in shaping your business is crucial.

As entrepreneurs, launching a business goes beyond merely offering a product or service—it's about making informed decisions and establishing a brand that resonates with your customers. To sell a product or service successfully, you must first craft a compelling story that speaks to the aspirations and dreams of those around you—and that's where branding comes into play!

Now, you're probably wondering, what exactly is branding? But before we discuss the intricacies of branding, let me share a bit about my journey. From an early age, I was driven by two passions: fashion and hip-hop. Little did I know these interests would shape my path as an entrepreneur. Fresh out of high school, I harbored grand aspirations of becoming a fashion designer and applied to the Fashion Institute of Technology in New York—only to face rejection. However, that setback turned out to be a blessing in disguise.

Fast forward a few years later, I decided to give fashion another shot and teamed up with my business partner to launch our own clothing brand. Armed with just $500 and a vision, we hit the streets, selling T-shirts out of the trunk of my car. Though seemingly simple, our inaugural design, the Bellargo boy T-shirt, carried a profound message: a tribute to hip-hop culture and a symbol of breaking barriers, much like hip-hop did in its early days. It represented my resilience and belief in an idea that was here to stay.

Starting a clothing brand from scratch was no easy feat. Initially, I had to distribute shirts for free and persuade influential individuals in my city to wear my designs.

In 2004, with strategic maneuvers and relentless effort, I managed to showcase our Bellargo boy T-shirt on a local rapper and friend named Gillie, who has since become a prominent figure in the industry.

This catapulted Bellargo into a household name in Philly and across the East Coast. The same individuals I once sought approval from were now seeking out our brand. Bellargo's association with hip-hop culture solidified its position as a favorite among top celebrities like Nicki Minaj, Meek Mill, Lil Uzi, PnB Rock, and many more.

When I say I went from selling shirts out of my car trunk to achieving seven figures, it's a testament to the transformative power of branding. With my background in business and branding, I expanded my horizons to other entrepreneurial ventures. In 2017, I had the opportunity to design merchandise for PnB Rock's *Catch These Vibes* album, providing merch for his tour, managing his e-commerce shop, and overseeing on-the-ground merch logistics.

Thanks to branding, my success goes beyond just starting a clothing brand; I am fostering a community and leaving a lasting legacy. This is why I'm deeply passionate about emphasizing the significance of branding in entrepreneurship.

Most of us understand why branding is paramount. Just imagine walking into a crowded room—how do you stand out? That's where branding comes in.

So, let's break it down! What exactly is branding? Think of branding as the personality of your business—it's what sets you apart, making you memorable and irresistibly attractive to your customers.

But here's the kicker: branding isn't merely about surface appeal. Branding is about defining who you are, what you stand for, and why you matter. It's about storytelling and sharing your passion, values, and mission with the world. You are crafting a love letter to your customers, telling them why they should choose you over everyone else. It encompasses everything from your logo and colors to your messaging and customer experience.

Remember to stay authentic and genuine in your brand. Authenticity is the cornerstone of effective branding, building trust and credibility with your audience.

And the best part? When branding is executed effectively, the sales start pouring in like never before. Because when people connect with your brand, they're not just purchasing a product or service; they're investing in a lifestyle, a vibe, and a complete experience.

Branding is your best tool for propelling your business growth, engaging with your audience, and turning your dreams into reality.

Let's uncover the power of storytelling, passion, and creativity in driving your business idea forward and realizing your full potential through the magic of branding.

How a Person Brands

Branding isn't just for businesses; individuals can brand themselves, too. Personal branding is about defining who you are, what you stand for, and how you want to be perceived by others. It's a chance to showcase your unique skills, strengths, and passions in a way that resonates with your audience.

Like businesses, individuals can use visual elements such as logos and colors to establish their brand. However, personal branding goes beyond visuals to encompass everything from your online presence and social media activity to your interactions with others.

Ultimately, personal branding allows you to build a reputation, becoming known for who you are and what you do best. Whether you're a freelancer, a job seeker, or an aspiring influencer, personal branding can help you stand out in a competitive market and attract opportunities.

The Power of Storytelling

Storytelling is a powerful tool in branding. It's how you bring your brand to life and connect with your audience on a deeper level. Stories can evoke emotions, inspire action, and forge meaningful connections.

Compelling storytelling is about more than just sharing facts and figures. You must also craft a narrative that resonates with your audience's hopes, dreams, and aspirations. This includes tapping into universal themes and experiences to create a shared sense of belonging and understanding.

Storytelling allows you to humanize your brand—to show the people behind the products, the passion behind the process, and the purpose behind the mission.

In today's digital age, storytelling has never been more critical. With so much noise and competition in the market, stories cut through the clutter and capture people's attention. Whether through social media posts, blog articles, or video content, storytelling allows you to engage your audience in meaningful ways and build lasting relationships.

In essence, storytelling is the heart of branding. It's how you create connections, inspire action, and leave a lasting impression. So, whether you're a business or an individual, harness the power of storytelling to elevate your brand and make a meaningful impact on the world.

Now that we've explored the foundational elements of branding, it's time to put theory into practice. As you embark on your entrepreneurial journey, remember that branding is not just a set of guidelines or rules. It's a living, breathing entity that grows and evolves with your business.

Stay true to your values, craft compelling stories, and engage with your audience authentically. Embrace the power of branding to differentiate yourself, build trust, and create lasting connections with your customers.

As you navigate the ever-changing entrepreneurship landscape, remember that your brand is your most valuable asset. Nurture it, refine it, and let it shine brightly in the crowded marketplace.

With passion, creativity, and a strong brand identity, you have the power to transform your business into a thriving success story. So, go forth and conquer the world of branding. Your journey to entrepreneurial greatness awaits!

Remember, your brand is your legacy—make it unforgettable!

Teen Designer, Orin pictured with Cash Cobain showcasing her Dream Team Jersey

GROWTH WORK
BRAND BRILLIANCE: CRAFTING YOUR UNIQUE IDENTITY

Unleash your creativity and define your brand's identity with this interactive worksheet. Get ready to stand out and shine in the competitive world of entrepreneurship!

What is the story behind your brand?

Take some time to reflect on the story behind your brand. What motivated you to start your business, and what values and principles does your brand stand for? Write a narrative that captures the essence of your brand's journey and purpose.

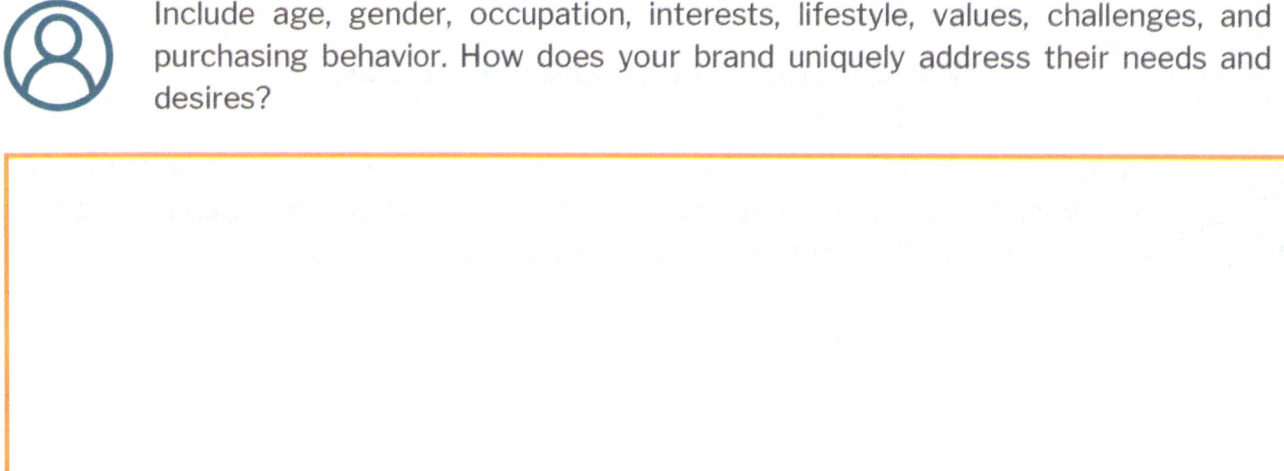

GROWTH WORK
BRAND BRILLIANCE: CRAFTING YOUR UNIQUE IDENTITY

Create your ideal customer avatar.

Include age, gender, occupation, interests, lifestyle, values, challenges, and purchasing behavior. How does your brand uniquely address their needs and desires?

What will your brand logo look like?

Create a visual symbol or logo that represents your brand. Your logo should be distinctive and memorable, reflecting the essence of your brand.

PRO TIP

Keep your design simple and versatile. Use Canva's logo maker tools to create a unique logo for your brand. Visit Canva.com/logos.

GROWTH WORK
BRAND BRILLIANCE: CRAFTING YOUR UNIQUE IDENTITY

What are your brand colors?

Select the colors that will represent your brand visually. Consider the emotions and impressions you want to convey and choose colors that align with your brand's personality and message. Visit Canva.com/colors/color-meanings to choose the right colors.

What fonts will you use for your brand?

Choose fonts that complement and enhance your brand's visual identity and personality, convey your message effectively, and can be easily read. Go to Canva.com/learn/best-free-fonts to help you decide on which font is right for you.

What's the voice of your brand messaging that you'll use in social media?

Define the tone and style of communication that will characterize your brand's messaging. Are you friendly and approachable, or professional and authoritative? Determine the best voice for your target audience and use it consistently in your communications.

GROWTH WORK
BRAND BRILLIANCE: CRAFTING YOUR UNIQUE IDENTITY

Write a love letter to your customers.

This love letter to your customers should express appreciation for their support and loyalty. It should highlight what makes your brand unique and why it stands out from the competition.

You can include elements such as your brand's mission, values, commitment to quality, and any special offers or benefits you provide your customers. The letter should be heartfelt and genuine, aiming to strengthen the relationship between your brand and its audience.

GROWTH WORK
CREATE YOUR BRAND GUIDE

What Is a Brand Guide?

A brand guide is a set of rules that explains how your brand looks and feels. It ensures that everything about your brand looks the same everywhere, which helps people recognize and trust your business. Consistency in branding is key to building a recognizable and trustworthy brand.

For example, The Boss Up Brand uses a specific brand guide to maintain consistency and professionalism across all its materials.

Elements of a Brand Guide:

1. Start with a Primary Logo: Your primary logo is the main symbol of your brand. It should be used consistently across all your brand's materials. For example, The Boss Up brand uses a specific logo that is always the same to maintain brand recognition.

2. Choose a Color Palette: The color palette consists of three to five primary colors representing your brand. All marketing materials should use these colors to maintain a cohesive look. Each color has a Hex code consisting of a "#" and six numbers that you'll need to write down. For instance, the Boss Up brand uses Pumpkin Orange (#F9943C), Dark Teal (#31677B), and Black (#000000) as its primary colors.

3. Create a Tagline: A tagline is a short, catchy phrase summarizing your brand's essence. It's a quick way to communicate your brand's message. The Boss Up brand's tagline, "The Official Guide to Teen Entrepreneurship," effectively captures its mission.

4. Select Fonts: Fonts are the styles of headers and body text you use in your branding materials. Make sure they are easy to read and match your brand's style. Consistency in fonts helps maintain a cohesive look. For example, the Boss Up brand uses "Futura" for headers and "Libre Franklin" for body text.

Check out the examples on the next page to see what we use for the "Boss Up!" brand. Then, head over to Canva to create your own brand guide using the provided template!

GROWTH WORK
CREATE YOUR BRAND GUIDE

BRAND GUIDELINE EXAMPLE FOR THE BOSS UP BRAND

PRIMARY LOGO
BOSS UP!

TAGLINE

THE OFFICIAL GUIDE TO
TEEN ENTREPRENEURSHIP

COLOR PALETTE

PUMPKIN ORANGE   **DARK TEAL**   **BLACK**

#F9943C   #31677B   #000000

FONTS

HEADER
FUTURA - BOLD
ABCDEFGHIJKLMNOPQRSTUVWXYZ
abcdefghijklmnopqrstuvwxyz

SUBHEADER
FUTURA
ABCDEFGHIJKLMNOPQRSTUVWXYZ
abcdefghijklmnopqrstuvwxyz

BODY
Libre Franklin
ABCDEFGHIJKLMNOPQRSTUVWXYZ
abcdefghijklmnopqrstuvwxyz

  **USE QR CODE FOR ACCESS TO YOUR CANVA ASSIGNMENTS**

GROWTH WORK
SAMPLE OF THE BRAND GUIDE TEMPLATE ON CANVA

PRIMARY LOGO

TAGLINE

<INSERT TAGLINE HERE>

FONTS

HEADINGS
BEBAS NEUE CYRILLIC

SUBHEADINGS
BEBAS NEU

Body Copy
Montserrat

COLOR

HOT PINK **BLUE** **WHITE** **BLACK** **GREY**
#ED0091 **#48BFDF** **#FFFFFF** **#000000** **#D6CFD2**

MOODBOARD

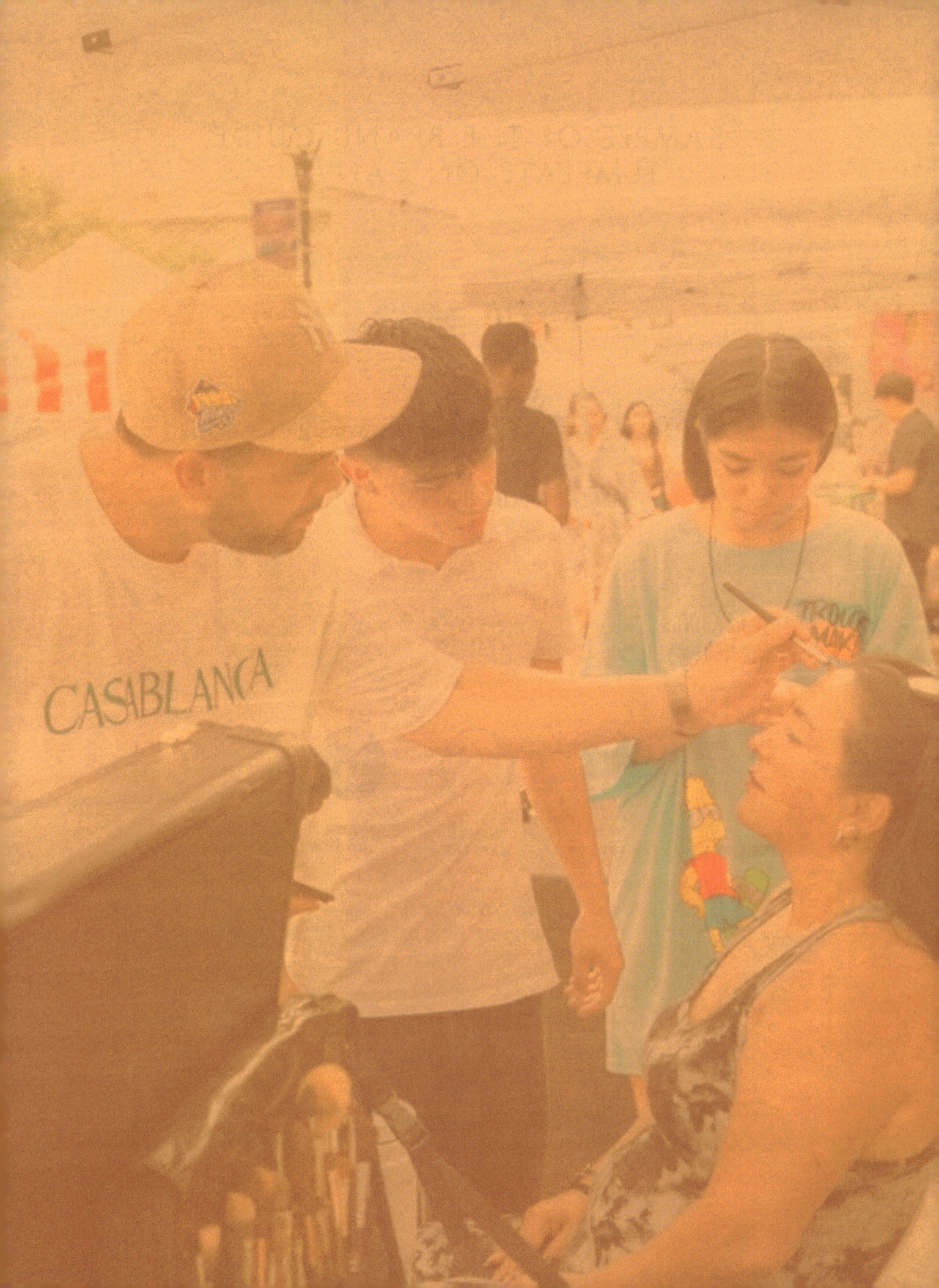

EXCERPT FROM TEEN MAGAZINE SUMMER 2024 EDITION

Meet Kwan Holmes: The Creative Mind Behind Munyun

By Mia Mack

Introducing Kwan Holmes, the 18-year-old fashion designer behind Munyun. With a passion for creating unique and standout clothing, Kwan is making waves in the fashion world with his distinct approach to design.

Fueled by a desire to break away from the norm and stand out from the crowd, Kwan launched Munyun to create outfits that matched his personal taste. Tired of wearing the same clothing as everyone else, he set out to carve his own path in the fashion industry.

At first, Kwan was uncertain whether his distinct approach would be noticed, but as he continued to post more products, he gained trust in his brand. One of his more recent designs features the Joker on the back, complete with his recognizable laugh and the Munyun logo. The name Munyun itself represents the importance of money in our lives--a motivator that drives us to keep pushing forward.

Kwan's journey with Munyun began with a bang as he launched his brand at a Lauryn Hill performance, where he sold out of his clothing and made a significant profit. This early success served as validation for Kwan, encouraging him to stay true to his passion and continue creating unique designs. "After I sold out at the concert, it showed me that I should stick with this."

He is supported by both family and friends, including his long-standing friend Justin, with whom he runs the business.

Kwan is determined to turn his vision into reality. Starting with little, he works tirelessly to create something out of nothing, fueled by his passion and courage. "I wanted something to stand out and be different from other people."

With Munyun, Kwan Holmes is not just creating clothing; he's creating a movement. A movement that celebrates individuality, creativity, and the drive to succeed against all odds.

CHAPTER 5
PRODUCT SOURCING & BUDGETING

So, you have an understanding of the Importance of budgeting, profit, and loss. Now, let's elevate our game and explore the world of product sourcing and budgeting. Understanding these aspects is crucial for taking your business to the next level.

5 PRODUCT SOURCING & BUDGETING

Welcome to the chapter where you level up and truly "Boss Up." We're diving into the world of product sourcing and budgeting. This is where you start making smart business deals, managing your money, and turning savvy budgeting into a profitable venture.

Remember your vision board? Now those dreams will start to take shape. In this chapter, we'll guide you through the essentials of sourcing the best products at the right prices and creating a budget that keeps your spending in check while maximizing your earnings.

Amani Crosby, 15, Owner of Kapture Kuture

Making Smart Business Deals
You're stepping into the role of a true entrepreneur. This means identifying the best suppliers, negotiating great deals, and ensuring the quality of your products. You'll learn how to source items that not only appeal to your target audience but also fit within your budget. Knowing how to strike a good deal is key to keeping costs low and profits high.

Managing Your Money
Effective money management is at the heart of any successful business. We'll teach you how to create and stick to a budget, ensuring that you don't spend more than you make. You'll understand the importance of tracking your expenses and income so you can make informed financial decisions. Smart budgeting helps you allocate funds where they're needed most and save for future growth.

Knowing who your customers are and what they need will help you make informed choices that meet their expectations and enhance their satisfaction.

The Big Flip: Turning Investments into Profits
The ultimate goal is to make your money work for you. By the end of this chapter, you'll be equipped with the knowledge to turn every dollar you invest into a profitable return. We'll show you how to calculate your costs, set the right prices for your products, and ensure that every sale contributes to your bottom line.

Get ready to transform your entrepreneurial dreams from your vision board into a successful reality. This chapter is your blueprint for making strategic decisions that will help you grow your business, maximize your profits, and truly "Boss Up."

Wholesalers vs. Retailers

As the CEO and head buyer of your company, it's time to make your first of many deals to come. Understanding the distinction between wholesalers and retailers is essential for making informed sourcing decisions.

Wholesalers sell products in large quantities at lower prices per unit. They often sell to businesses rather than individual consumers.
- Advantages: Lower costs per unit can boost profit margins, ideal for bulk inventory.
- Considerations: They often have minimum order requirements. Ensure you have storage space, a budget, and a business license if needed. Check local requirements for wholesale purchases.

Specialized Wholesalers offer a broader range of products for specific needs. For example, apparel businesses can explore Sanmar, S&S Activewear, and Alphabroder for clothing and accessories.
- Advantage: They provide a wide variety of high-quality products, ideal for specific business needs.
- Consideration: They may have higher minimum order requirements and prices. A business license is often required for purchases. Check local regulations.

Online Marketplaces and Trade Directories, like Alibaba, ThomasNet, and Wholesale Central, connect you with many wholesalers and manufacturers.
- Advantage: Access a vast array of suppliers and products worldwide, offering numerous options for deals and unique items.
- Consideration: Vet suppliers for reliability and quality. Shipping times and costs can vary. A business license may be required for wholesale purchases; check local regulations.

Retailers sell products directly to consumers, usually in smaller quantities at higher prices per unit compared to wholesalers.
- Advantages: Retailers are usually local and offer convenience and smaller order sizes, which is ideal for testing new products or if you have limited storage space.
- Considerations: Higher costs per unit can reduce your profit margins.

Key Factors to Consider

When researching wholesale and retail options, think about these important factors, as they directly affect your COGS, which stands for: Cost of Goods Sold. These factors include your pricing, profit, and profit margin:

- Product Quality: Make sure the products are good quality and won't break easily or look cheap. Always ask for a sample to check the quality before buying in bulk. This will reduce returns and keep customers happy, which boosts your profit margins.

- Pricing: Compare suppliers to find the best deals. Lower COGS increases profit margins. Look for bulk discounts.

- Shipping: Include shipping costs in your COGS. Ensure timely delivery to avoid stockouts. If importing, consider customs fees, as they can impact costs and profit margins.

Customer Service is the final consideration when choosing suppliers with good reputations and positive reviews. Good customer service can help you solve problems quickly, reduce costs related to returns, and keep your customers happy, which indirectly supports stable profit margins.

Once you've identified potential wholesalers or retailers, building a strong, mutually beneficial relationship with them can offer added advantages, such as early access to new products or more flexible payment options. These benefits can help both you and your supplier thrive and contribute to your business's success.

Finding the best deals and sourcing quality supplies at competitive prices is critical for any business. You can research wholesalers online for whatever business you may be starting. There are specialized wholesalers for nearly every industry, and a quick web search can help you find the right suppliers to meet your business needs.

Use platforms like Amazon to research market trends. By analyzing sales data and customer reviews, you can identify popular products and market opportunities. This research helps you understand what products are in demand and can guide you in making smart decisions for your business.

Creating A Budget

Once you've sourced your products, it's time to create a detailed sourcing budget that outlines all the expenses directly related to acquiring your goods and necessary equipment.

When it comes to budgeting, meticulous planning is key. Map out all your expenses, from sourcing to marketing to overhead costs, and be as detailed as possible. Prioritize essential expenses that drive your business's growth while keeping a close eye on your profit margins.

For some people, math, in general, can sometimes feel overwhelming, but don't let it intimidate you. Understanding key formulas is crucial for turning your business dreams into reality and maintaining both financial health and mental well-being. Let's break down why grasping these concepts is vital to your success.

In business, you're not just serving your customers and community—you're also aiming for **"The Big Flip,"** which is your profit. It is essential, and here's why:

- **Financial Freedom and Stability:** Profit helps you live how you want by funding your activities, travel, and interests. It also gives you a steady income to cover your daily expenses and maintain your lifestyle.

- **Growth and Flexibility:** Profit lets you invest in your business to expand, upgrade, or improve your products and services. It also gives you the freedom to adapt to changes, seize new opportunities, and make smart decisions without risking your business.

- **Less Stress and More Confidence**: Having profit reduces money-related stress, making your life more balanced and less anxious. It also boosts your confidence, helps you make better decisions, and gives you a more positive outlook on your work and life.

If you don't monitor your profit, you might not realize when your expenses start to outweigh your revenue, which can lead to financial trouble and potentially threaten the stability of your business. Regularly tracking your profit helps you catch issues early, make necessary adjustments, and keep your business on a successful path.

You're about to learn the essentials of staying profitable using simple math. These are the building blocks of ensuring your business isn't just running but thriving. With these tools, you'll understand how to set your prices wisely and keep your business on track. Let's dive in and make sure you're flipping those numbers to your advantage!

The Math Has to Math

Here's the deal: Math may not be your thing, but it's actually about to be your secret weapon. Think of it like having X-ray vision in the business world – you'll see opportunities others miss and dodge mistakes that could trip you up. When you understand the numbers, you can make smarter decisions, like knowing how much to spend on materials, setting the right prices, and figuring out your profits.

We've made it easy to follow so you can see where your hard-earned money is going and how it's growing. With these skills, you'll be able to manage your budget, make wise investments, and ensure your business is on the path to success.

Understanding Key Financial Terms

Before diving into the key factors to consider when researching wholesale options, it's important to understand a few financial terms that will influence your business decisions:

- **Cost of Goods Sold (COGS):** This is the money you spend to buy and/or make the products and services you sell.

- **Pricing:** This is the amount of money you charge your customers for your products or services. Setting the right price helps you cover your costs and make a profit.

- **Revenue:** This is the total amount of money your business brings in from selling products or services. It's the income generated before any expenses are subtracted.

- **Profit (The Big Flip):** This is the money you make after covering all your expenses. It's called "The Big Flip" because it's like flipping your investment into profit.

We'll get into how to calculate these concepts easily shortly. Understanding these concepts will help you make smart choices about which suppliers to choose and how to price your products or services to achieve your financial goals.

This may feel like a lot of information, and you might be feeling a bit overwhelmed right now. It can be hard to see how all these pieces fit together and apply to your business. To make things clearer and more manageable, we'll move on to practical examples. These will show you how to apply these concepts in real-world scenarios to help you understand how to use this information to make smart decisions for your own business, step by step.

Example of a Product-Based Business

Imagine you're running an online business designing and selling your own cool T-shirts, hoodies, and other urban wear. Instead of making the clothes from scratch, you buy pre-made ones in bulk and customize them with your own designs using a heat press machine. You design and create the T-shirts once and can sell the same design multiple times. This means you don't have to redo the work for each sale, saving you a lot of time!

Once your designs are made, they can be sold repeatedly without extra effort. This makes it easier to grow your business by focusing on marketing and increasing production.

Wholesalers or Specialty Wholesalers: These companies sell pre-made clothing items like T-shirts and hoodies in large quantities at lower prices. They usually have minimum order requirements, so plan your purchases to fit your needs while keeping costs in check.

Let's get into the money:

Cost of Goods Sold (COGS):
- T-Shirts: Buy in bulk from a wholesaler at $5 each x 50 T-shirts = $250.
- Heat Press Machine: To transfer designs onto the T-shirts = $150 (one-time cost).
- Supplies: Transfer paper, custom tags, and shipping supplies. $50.
- Shipping: From U.S. wholesaler = $25.

  COGS = $475

Pricing: Check out what similar T-shirts are selling for online. Let's say $30 is a good starting price.

Revenue: If you sell 50 T-shirts for $30 each, you'll make $1,500.

The Big Flip: Subtract what you spent from what you made. $1,500 - $475 = **$1,025 profit!**

Now, don't spend that so quickly. Flip it immediately by buying more shirts and investing in your marketing. Your online store operates 24/7, making sales even while you're not actively working, creating opportunities for passive income. By reinvesting your profits wisely, you can continue to grow your business and increase your pricing and profits over time.

Example of a Service-Based Business

Imagine you own a computer and are skilled in digital services like graphic design, social media management, or video editing. You can turn these skills into a business by offering your services to YouTubers, small businesses, or individuals looking to enhance their online presence. With minimal upfront costs, you can start managing multiple clients simultaneously, making this a flexible and lucrative business.

Retailers: In this case, we'll use online platforms and subscriptions for your digital services. Invest in software subscriptions and marketing materials to promote your business.

Cost of Goods Sold (COGS):
- Software Subscriptions (Retailers): Essential tools like Adobe Creative Suite, Canva Pro, CapCut, Wix (for your website), and Asana (for project management) = $200 per month
- Marketing Materials: Business cards printing = $25
- Initial Utilities: Internet and other necessary utilities = $50

  Total COGS = $275

Pricing: Look at what other digital service providers in your area charge. For example, you might decide to charge $500 per month for social media management, which includes graphic design services, and $400 per month for video editing services.

Revenue:

Services Booked:
- Social Media Management: 5 clients x $500 = $2,500
- Video Editing: 3 clients x $400 = $1200

  $3,700 in Revenue

The Big Flip: $3,700 (Revenue) - $275 (COGS) = **$3,425 In profit !**

Save and Reinvest: Flip a portion of your profit by investing in marketing, purchasing additional software, upgrading your tools, or taking courses to improve your skills. Use part of your profits to create a professional website, enhance your social media presence, or run online ads. The more people who know about your services, the more likely you are to attract new clients. Clients come and go, so these investments can help you build a pipeline to keep your client list full!

Example of a Product + Service-Based Business

Imagine you love styling intricate braids, stylish weaves, and creating custom wigs. In this business, you offer personalized hair services and products. Many clients prefer to bring their own hair, paying for your service and skill. However, you can also sell hair under your brand, offering convenience and quality that clients trust. They have the option to purchase your service, your product, or both.

Wholesalers & Retailers: In this case, we'll use both.

Cost of Goods Sold (COGS):

- Hair Products and Accessories (Wholesaler): Synthetic or human hair, silk bonnets and packaging. = $200
- Tools (Retailer): Combs, clips, scissors, and a wig stand and wig head = $150
- Initial Rent/Utilities: If working from home = $50
- Shipping: From U.S. wholesaler = $25

    Total COGS = $425

Pricing: Look at what other hairstylists in your area charge. For example, you might charge $100 for a basic braid style, $250 for an intricate design, $200 for a weave, and $300 for a custom wig. Offer clients the option to buy hair directly from you.

- Pack of 3 Bundles of Synthetic Hair: $20
- Pack of 2 Bundles of Human Hair: $300 alone or $250 with a service

Show Customer Appreciation: Offer silk bonnets as a free gift for clients who spend over $200 on services.

Revenue:

Styling Services Booked:
- Basic Braid Styles: 10 x $100 = $1,000
- Intricate Braid Designs: 5 x $250 = $1,250
- Weaves: 3 x $200 = $600
- Custom Wigs: 2 x $300 = $600

    $3,450 in Services

Hair Sold:
- Synthetic Hair: 5 x $20 = $100
- Human Hair with Service: 2 x $250 = $500
- Human Hair Alone: 1 x $300 = $300

    $900 in Product Sales

Totaling $4,350 in Revenue

The Big Flip: $4,350 (Revenue) - $425 (COGS) = **$3,925 profit!**

Save and Reinvest: Flip a portion to reinvest in your business, using marketing to attract more clients and looking into renting a space to grow. This business can grow quickly, so be ready!

The Continuous Flip

Now that you've calculated your initial start-up flip, you know what you have to do to keep the momentum going. The importance of this flip cannot be overstated; it's the foundation for your business's financial health. Knowing your ongoing monthly expenses is essential to keeping your business thriving.

Here are some pointers to guide you:

- **Inventory Management:** Ensure you have enough stock or materials to make your goods to meet demand without overstocking or overproducing, which ties up cash.
- **Marketing Expenses:** Allocate funds for advertising, promotions, and digital marketing to attract and retain customers.
- **Operational Costs:** Include utilities, rent, software subscriptions, and other necessary expenses to keep your business running smoothly.
- **Logistics:** Consider shipping, transportation, and storage costs, especially when selling physical products.
- **Unexpected Expenses:** Set aside a portion of your budget for unforeseen costs like equipment repairs or emergency purchases.

As you calculate your costs, consider your pricing strategy to ensure your prices cover expenses while providing a profit margin. As you track these expenses, remember the importance of reinvesting in your business for growth.

You must revisit this budget, adjust the lists and expenses as needed, and refine your strategy as you crystallize your goals. Remember your vision and mission to ensure every expense aligns with your business goals. In the next chapter, we'll address sourcing and, later, marketing. Both are crucial aspects of your business that will require careful budget planning. These elements ensure your business operates efficiently and effectively, allowing you to continue growing and securing that steady bag.

Finally, revisit your vision board regularly. Reflect on your goals, the life you want to live, and what achieving that will cost. Remember, your goals and aspirations may evolve as you grow and learn more about your business journey. Stay adaptable and keep your vision clear as you move forward.

Congratulations! You've officially entered Boss Mode! Let's go!

CASE STUDIES

Now that you've learned the basics of sourcing and budgeting, let's explore two case studies that will give us an even clearer understanding.

Meet Maya

Maya is a seventeen-year-old entrepreneur venturing into the house cleaning business. While Maya's expertise lies in cleaning homes, she understands the need for essential supplies like cleaning agents, brushes, mops, and vacuums to deliver exceptional service to her clients.

Maya begins her product sourcing journey by researching wholesale options for cleaning supplies. After comparing prices, she opts to purchase her supplies in bulk from Costco to benefit from discounted rates. Buying in bulk allows Maya to lower her costs and increase her profits.

In her budget, Maya sets aside funds for cleaning supplies, equipment maintenance, transportation, and marketing expenses. She ensures that all overhead costs are considered to maintain a healthy profit margin.

Meet Jamal

Now, let's introduce Jamal, an eighteen-year-old entrepreneur passionate about fashion who has started his own apparel company specializing in custom-designed T-shirts. Jamal recognizes the importance of sourcing high-quality materials at affordable prices for his business's success.

Jamal begins sourcing materials by researching wholesale suppliers for blank shirts and screen printing services. After evaluating prices and quality, he chooses to purchase shirts from Sanmar and utilize screen printing services from FM Expressions. This strategic sourcing approach allows him to create custom-designed T-shirts at competitive rates.

In his budget, Jamal factors in costs for materials, screen printing services, equipment (such as a heat press), packaging materials, promotional items, and website fees. By accounting for all expenses, Jamal ensures a healthy profit margin while offering competitive prices to his customers.

In conclusion, young entrepreneurs like Maya and Jamal have paved the way for their success by mastering product sourcing and budgeting. They grasp the significance of sourcing quality products economically and crafting a comprehensive budget to steer their business operations. With determination, strategic planning, and sharp business acumen, they are poised to elevate their entrepreneurial journey to new horizons!

GROWTH WORK
NAVIGATING PRODUCT SOURCING

This exercise will guide you through budgeting, sourcing your products, and tracking your profit and loss to secure a big bag without any holes.

Do you know your business needs? What supplies or materials are essential for delivering your services or creating your products? Refer to your earlier exercises on identifying your business needs and adjusting accordingly.

Which option—wholesalers or retailers—best fits your business model? Consider the insights from your earlier exercises on understanding your target market and business model.

Research wholesale options. Where can you find the best deals for what you need? Refer to your earlier market research and adjust your findings based on new insights.

GROWTH WORK
NAVIGATING PRODUCT SOURCING

Evaluate retail options. Which retail options align with your needs and budget? Consider any changes in budget or target market preferences since your earlier exercises.

How will you distribute your funds wisely? Refer to your earlier budgeting exercise and make any necessary adjustments based on new information.

Are you feeling confident about your budget and taking the steps to place your first orders? Why or why not?

GROWTH WORK
BUDGETING YOUR BIZ NEEDS

What will your first month of business expenses include?

Inventory and Raw Materials:
Product-specific materials and product packaging, etc.

_____ $ _____
_____ $ _____
_____ $ _____
_____ $ _____
_____ $ _____

Budget Total $ _____

Marketing
Website, advertising, business cards, brochures, flyers, and promo merch, etc.

_____ $ _____
_____ $ _____
_____ $ _____
_____ $ _____
_____ $ _____

Budget Total $ _____

Operations and Equipment:
Tools and machinery, safety equipment, maintenance supplies, etc.

_____ $ _____
_____ $ _____
_____ $ _____
_____ $ _____
_____ $ _____

Budget Total $ _____

Logistics and Shipping:
Shipping boxes and envelopes, packing materials, labels, etc.

_____ $ _____
_____ $ _____
_____ $ _____
_____ $ _____
_____ $ _____

Budget Total $ _____

Other:

_____ $ _____
_____ $ _____
_____ $ _____
_____ $ _____
_____ $ _____

Budget Total $ _____

Other:

_____ $ _____
_____ $ _____
_____ $ _____
_____ $ _____
_____ $ _____

Budget Total $ _____

GROWTH WORK

THE BIG FLIP: COGS

Calculate your expenses: Cost of Item(s) Needed x Quantity = Total Expense

Item(s) Needed   Cost   Qty.   Expense

_____ $ [ ] x [ ] = $ [ ]

Item(s) Needed   Cost   Qty   Expense

_____ $ [ ] x [ ] = $ [ ]

Item(s) Needed   Cost   Qty   Expense

_____ $ [ ] x [ ] = $ [ ]

Item(s) Needed   Cost   Qty   Expense

_____ $ [ ] x [ ] = $ [ ]

Item(s) Needed   Cost   Qty   Expense

_____ $ [ ] x [ ] = $ [ ]

Add up your total start-up expenses $ [ ]

GROWTH WORK

THE BIG FLIP
REVENUE PROJECTIONS

 List your products or services, set prices, estimate the number sold, and calculate the total revenue to project your earnings for your new business.

Item(s)/Service(s)	Selling Price	Qty. Sold	Revenue
_____	$ _____	x _____	= $ _____
_____	$ _____	x _____	= $ _____
_____	$ _____	x _____	= $ _____
_____	$ _____	x _____	= $ _____
_____	$ _____	x _____	= $ _____

Add Up Your Total Revenue $ _____

Profit and Loss (P&L)

Did you profit, or are you losing money? Did you spend that $500 wisely? Calculate your profit or loss by subtracting total COG expenses from total revenue to find out.

REVENUE $ _____
- TOTAL COGS $ _____
PROFIT OR LOSS? $ _____

If you made a profit, awesome job! You're flipping that initial investment into a solid bag!
If you made a loss, don't stress—it's all part of the hustle. Reevaluate your spending and strategy, then recalculate your budget and expenses to find better ways to secure the bag. The goal is to flip your investment into profit. Keep grinding and refining your approach!

GROWTH WORK

SAMPLE SOURCE LIST
CANVA TEMPLATE

SOURCE LIST

PRODUCT :
DESCRIPTION :
COMPANY :
EMAIL :
PHONE :

PRODUCT :
DESCRIPTION :
COMPANY :
EMAIL :
PHONE :

PRODUCT :
DESCRIPTION :
COMPANY :
EMAIL :
PHONE :

PRODUCT :
DESCRIPTION :
COMPANY :
EMAIL :
PHONE :

PRODUCT :
DESCRIPTION :
COMPANY :
EMAIL :
PHONE :

PRODUCT :
DESCRIPTION :
COMPANY :
EMAIL :
PHONE :

PRODUCT :
DESCRIPTION :
COMPANY :
EMAIL :
PHONE :

PRODUCT :
DESCRIPTION :
COMPANY :
EMAIL :
PHONE :

GROWTH WORK

SAMPLE SOURCE DOCUMENT
CANVA TEMPLATE

SOURCE DOC

ITEM	IMAGE	LINK
(Type here)		(Type here)
(Type here)		(Type here)
(Type here)		(Type here)

USE QR CODE FOR ACCESS TO YOUR CANVA ASSIGNMENTS

EXCERPT FROM TEEN MAGAZINE SUMMER 2024 EDITION

Meet Orin Ogle: The Teen Entrepreneur Redefining Streetwear with DTB

By: Sarai Gordon

Hip Hop Legend Lauryn Hill holding Orin Ogle's Shirt

Introducing Orin Ogle, the 15-year-old fashion maverick behind DTB Clothing (Dreams Aren't Too Big Clothing). With a passion for fashion, Orin is taking the industry by storm with his cutting-edge streetwear brand.

Orin's journey in the fashion industry began at just 14 years old when he founded DTB Clothing, specializing in the latest fashion trends, particularly streetwear for teenagers. When asked about his journey, he went silent.

He has few words but a powerful impact on the fashion industry. Despite his young age, Orin had always been passionate about fashion and design, and he decided to turn his passion into a business after facing rejection from a previous venture.

Determined to prove that no dreams are too big, Orin forged ahead with DTB, and today, at only 15 years old, he continues to run his business successfully. With hit collections in his hometown of East Orange, Orin's clothing line constantly sells out, earning him a loyal following of fashion-forward teens. He uses his friends and fellow peers to model his work, which includes hoodies, sweatshirts, sweaters, tracksuits, and beanies.

A pivotal moment in Orin's career came when he had the opportunity to meet Lauryn Hill at the SWEP Fest in East Orange in 2023. Seizing the moment, Orin boldly approached Ms. Hill and requested that she take a picture in his signature shirt. The viral photo not only garnered attention on social media but also caught the eye of Dr. Jamila T. Davis, who shared the image with Ms. Hill. Impressed by Orin's courage and entrepreneurial spirit, Ms. Hill invited him and other student entrepreneurs to be vendors at her concert at the Prudential Center, where Orin sold out of his clothes.

Orin's fearless approach to networking and his willpower to succeed have not only propelled his brand to new heights but have also brought recognition and opportunities to his city. With DTB, Orin Ogle is proving that determination and hard work can get you wherever you want. His story serves as an inspiration to aspiring entrepreneurs everywhere. Keep an eye on Orin and DTB as they continue to redefine streetwear.

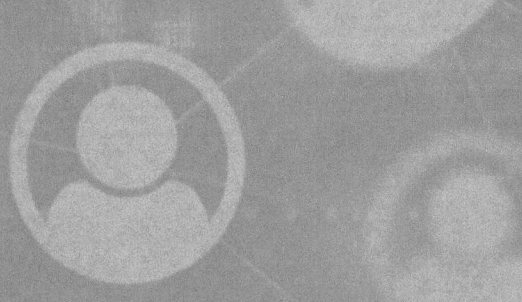

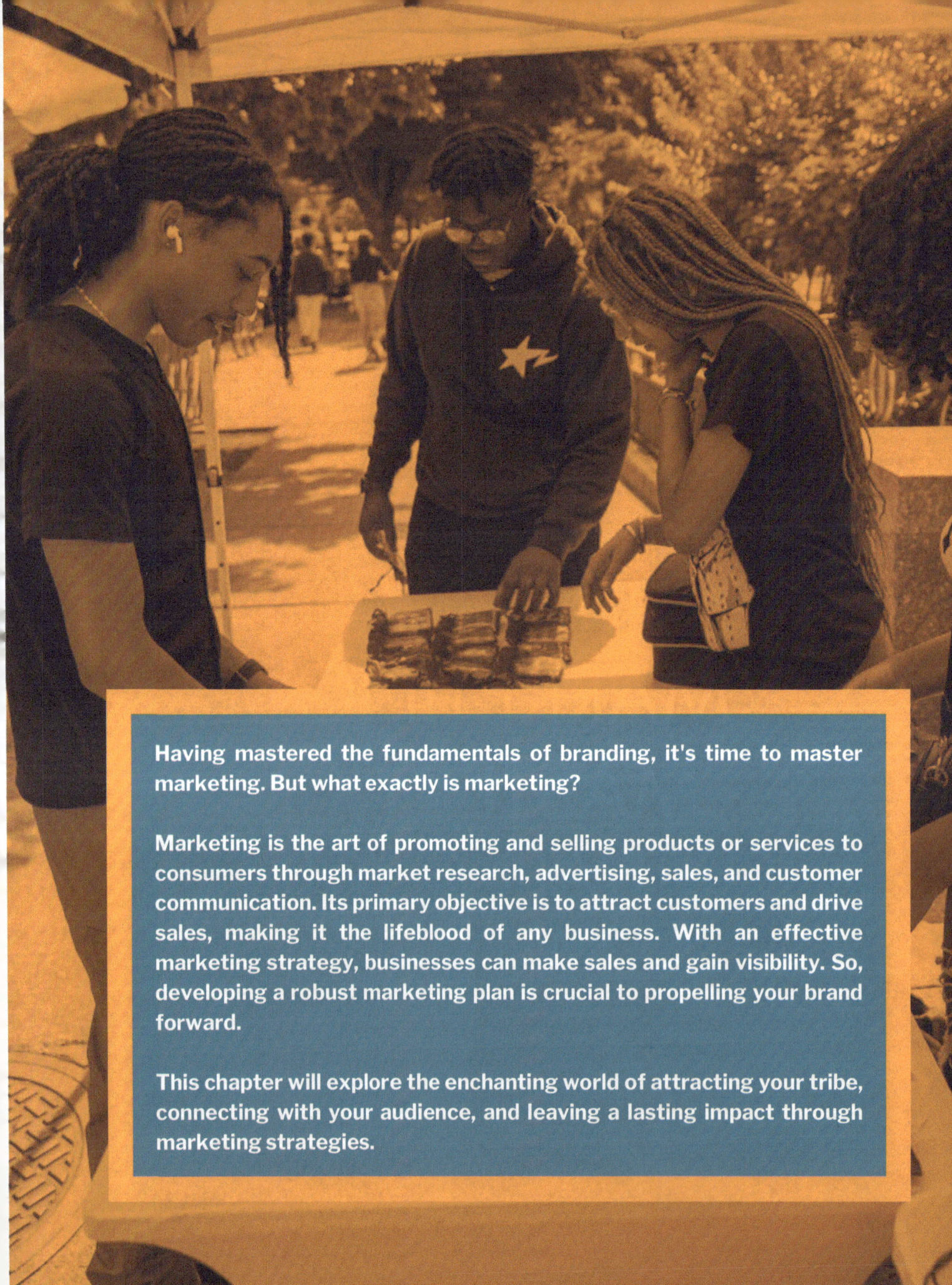

Having mastered the fundamentals of branding, it's time to master marketing. But what exactly is marketing?

Marketing is the art of promoting and selling products or services to consumers through market research, advertising, sales, and customer communication. Its primary objective is to attract customers and drive sales, making it the lifeblood of any business. With an effective marketing strategy, businesses can make sales and gain visibility. So, developing a robust marketing plan is crucial to propelling your brand forward.

This chapter will explore the enchanting world of attracting your tribe, connecting with your audience, and leaving a lasting impact through marketing strategies.

6 MARKETING MASTERY: CULTIVATING YOUR COMMUNITY

Before we proceed, it's essential to differentiate between **branding** and **marketing**. While branding focuses on creating a unique identity for a product, service, or company, marketing is about promoting and selling these offerings to consumers.

Branding establishes a strong brand image, values, and reputation, aiming to forge an emotional connection with customers and set the brand apart from competitors.

On the other hand, marketing involves tactics like advertisements and sales strategies to drive product visibility and sales. While marketing tactics may evolve over time, branding remains steadfast in building a consistent brand image.

Understanding Your Target Audience
The first step towards successful marketing is understanding your target market. Imagine launching a business selling customized sneakers. Who is your ideal customer? Are they sneaker enthusiasts always on the hunt for the latest trends? Or perhaps they are fashion-forward individuals looking to express their unique style? By identifying your target audience's demographics, interests, and shopping behaviors, you can effectively tailor your products and marketing efforts to resonate with them.

For example, suppose your research reveals that your target audience comprises environmentally conscious Gen Z sneaker enthusiasts. In that case, you can create sustainable designs and launch a marketing campaign centered on sustainability to attract like-minded customers.

Teen entrepreneur, Amani Crosby, makes greats strides in business with media news coverage for her fashion design business

Creating Compelling Marketing Strategies

Once you've defined your target market, the next step is to craft a strategic marketing plan that aligns with your audience's interests and addresses their needs. Dive deep into understanding what motivates your customers, empathize with their challenges, and showcase how your offerings can enhance their lives positively.

To tailor your marketing plan effectively, immerse yourself in understanding your customers' dreams and aspirations. By aligning your marketing messages with their ambitions and desires, you can effectively communicate how your brand meets their needs. For instance, if you're targeting environmentally conscious teens, highlight the eco-friendly features of your products.

Equally important is identifying your customers' pain points—the problems or frustrations they encounter daily. By positioning your products or services as solutions to these pain points, you can resonate with your audience and drive sales. For example, if your target customers are busy teens, emphasize how your time-saving solution simplifies their routines.

Once you've gained insight into your audience's desires and pain points, craft engaging messaging that speaks directly to them. Your marketing content should clearly articulate how your offerings address their needs and challenges, using language that resonates with their emotions and highlights the benefits of choosing your brand.

Diving into Digital Marketing

Selecting the proper channels to reach your target audience is critical. Consider their preferences and behaviors when choosing platforms. Whether it's social media platforms like Instagram and TikTok, email newsletters, influencer collaborations, or targeted advertising, opt for channels that align with how your audience consumes media. For instance, if your target customers are teenagers, focus on platforms like Snapchat and YouTube, where they spend a lot of time.

Creating captivating content is key to capturing your audience's attention. Develop high-quality content that educates, entertains, and inspires your audience. Whether it's blog posts, videos, infographics, or interactive quizzes, provide valuable content that resonates with your customers' interests and offers solutions to their challenges. By positioning yourself as a trusted source of information, you can establish credibility and foster loyalty among your teen customers.

Remember, marketing is all about building relationships. Engage with your customers on social media, respond to their comments and messages, and seek feedback on your products or services. Cultivating a sense of community and connection allows you to deepen brand loyalty and transform your teen customers into advocates for your brand.

By following these steps and implementing a targeted marketing strategy, you can effectively engage your target audience, drive conversations, and build a devoted customer base for your business.

Types of Digital Marketing

Understanding the distinctions between traditional and digital marketing is essential for crafting effective marketing strategies.

Traditional marketing encompasses channels like print media, television, radio, and direct mail. While still relevant in certain contexts, traditional marketing may lack precision and cost-effectiveness compared to digital marketing. On the other hand, digital marketing leverages platforms such as social media, email, search engines, and websites to engage target audiences. Digital marketing offers greater precision, measurability, and flexibility, making it ideal for teen entrepreneurs seeking to connect with their audience in today's digital landscape.

Let's explore the different forms of digital marketing and their benefits.

Social Media Marketing

Platforms like Instagram, TikTok, and Snapchat provide teen entrepreneurs a stage to showcase their offerings in visually appealing ways. Benefits include heightened brand visibility, direct engagement with audiences, and the potential for viral content.

Email Marketing

Email remains a potent channel for reaching and nurturing leads. Benefits include delivering personalized messages, building customer relationships, and driving conversations through targeted campaigns.

Search Engine Optimization (SEO)

SEO involves optimizing your website and content to rank higher in search results. Benefits include increased organic traffic, enhanced visibility, and credibility among audiences seeking relevant information or products.

Content Marketing

Creating and distributing valuable content to attract and engage a specific audience is the crux of content marketing. Benefits include establishing thought leadership, fostering customer trust, and driving website traffic through resources like blog posts and videos.

Influencer Marketing

Collaborating with influencers who resonate with your target audience can amplify your brand's message and reach. Benefits include access to a highly engaged audience, increased brand awareness, and authentic endorsements from trusted influencers.

Digital Advertising: In the fast-paced world of being a young entrepreneur, connecting with your audience correctly is essential to make your business successful. Luckily, as a teen entrepreneur, you've got a powerful weapon: digital advertising. Platforms like Facebook Ads, Google Ads, and ads on social media are fantastic ways to reach your audience and get them interested in what you're doing. Let's dig into how these ads can help your business and make your marketing dreams come true.

Facebook Ads: With over two billion people using Facebook, it's a huge platform to show off your business. You can use Facebook's detailed targeting options to reach specific groups of people based on things like their interests and behaviors. By using cool ad formats like images and videos, you can catch the eye of your audience. Facebook also gives you lots of info on how your ads are doing, so you can make them even better to get more results.

Google Ads: Google Ads (used to be called Google AdWords) lets you reach folks actively looking for stuff on Google. By bidding on keywords, you can ensure your ads appear at the top of search results. Google also has an extensive network of websites and apps like YouTube and Gmail, where you can put up display and video ads. Plus, Google gives you loads of data on how your ads are working, so you can change things up to get better results.

Ads on Social Media Platforms: Instagram, X, LinkedIn, and Pinterest are all great places for businesses to connect with their audience through ads. You can target users on these platforms based on things like what they're into and how they engage with content. Whether it's through sponsored posts or working with influencers, there are many ways to catch your audience's attention. And with the tools on these platforms, you can see how your ads are doing and make them even more effective.

By using Facebook ads, Google ads, and ads on social media, teen entrepreneurs can create cool and engaging ad campaigns that speak to their audience and get results. These digital advertising tools give you the power to connect with your audience, engage with them, and reach your marketing goals in today's competitive world.

Students pose with author Aisha Hall and Larry the Lending Lion

Return on Investment and Analytics

Now that you understand the power of digital ads, let's discuss something fundamental regarding marketing: ROI, which stands for Return on Investment.

Imagine you're investing in something, like buying ingredients to bake cookies. Now, you want to know if spending money on those ingredients was worth it, right?

Teen Entrepreneur, Khashearer proudly poses in front of merchandise at Teen Pop Up

That's where ROI comes in! Here's a simple way to think about it: ROI is like measuring how much bang you get for your buck.

Suppose you spend $10 on cookie ingredients and sell the cookies for $30. Your ROI is $20 ($30 - $10 = $20), meaning you made $20 more than you spent.

In marketing, it's the same idea. If you spend money on advertising or promoting your business, you want to ensure you get back more money than you put in. So, when we talk about **Return On Investment (ROI)** in marketing, we're looking at how much money we make from our marketing efforts compared to how much we spend. Here's where analytics come into play.

Analytics is the behind-the-scenes magic that helps us understand how our marketing works. It's like having a secret spy that collects data and tells us what's going on with our business. With analytics, we can track how many people visit our website, how long they stay, and whether they buy anything.

We can also see which ads or social media posts get the most clicks or engagement. This helps us determine what's working well and might need some tweaking.

Now that you're equipped with marketing principles, it's time to put them into practice! The upcoming exercises will help you craft a marketing plan tailored to your brand and social media assets to enhance visibility and brand recognition.

The more you experiment and test the market, the better you'll understand which marketing strategies work best for you. It's time to elevate your game and weave some marketing magic!

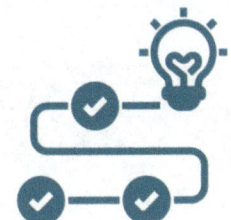

CASE STUDIES

Now that you've learned the fundamentals of marketing and building a community around your brand, let's dive into two case studies that demonstrate effective strategies.

Meet Taylor

Taylor, 16, is entrepreneur who started her custom phone case business, Case Craze, after realizing a gap in the market for personalized, trendy phone accessories. As she prepared for her first pop-up event, Taylor knew she needed a marketing strategy to generate excitement.

She focused on engaging her Instagram followers by posting polls where they could vote on designs and colors for limited-edition cases she would release at the event. Taylor also launched a giveaway, encouraging followers to tag friends for a chance to win a free custom case.

This helped her grow her follower base and build anticipation. Additionally, she collaborated with local influencers, who posted about her brand leading up to the event. By the time of the pop-up, the buzz she had created translated into high foot traffic, with many customers eager to purchase her exclusive designs. Taylor sold out of most of her stock and gained over 200 new followers, making the event a huge success.

Meet Carlos

Carlos, 17, was passionate about sustainability and launched a line of eco-friendly backpacks made from recycled materials. As he prepared for his first pop-up, Carlos crafted a marketing strategy that highlighted his brand's environmental focus.

He used Instagram to share the story of how his backpacks were made, emphasizing their eco-friendly impact. Carlos also partnered with a local environmental nonprofit to co-host an event promoting sustainable living, where his pop-up was featured. This collaboration helped him reach customers who aligned with his mission.

In the weeks before the event, Carlos shared behind-the-scenes videos and customer testimonials, creating buzz for his brand. On the day of the pop-up, Carlos attracted a crowd of customers who were drawn to his message, and he sold nearly all of his inventory. His success also earned attention from local media, boosting his visibility even further.

In conclusion, young entrepreneurs like Taylor and Carlos have achieved success by mastering the art of marketing and community engagement. They understood the importance of connecting with their audience, building anticipation, and aligning their strategies with their brand values. Through creative campaigns, strategic partnerships, and consistent social media engagement, they turned their marketing plans into tangible results. With determination, innovation, and a strong focus on cultivating their communities, they are well on their way to elevating their entrepreneurial ventures to new heights!

GROWTH WORK
PLAN YOUR MARKETING MAGIC

Get ready to elevate your business plan! This tool guides you in crafting a targeted marketing strategy to reach your audience and boost sales. Transfer your plan to the Canva template for marketing success!

Think back to your target audience. Who are the main people you want to sell to? Consider their age, interests, and needs.

Recall the avatar you created. What does this ideal customer look like? Describe their habits, preferences, and lifestyle in detail.

What marketing methods will you use to reach your customers? Consider which social media platforms or events will appeal to them.

GROWTH WORK
PLAN YOUR MARKETING MAGIC

What will be your sales strategy? How will you convince people to buy your product? What makes your approach stand out?

List specific actions to execute your sales strategy. For example, hosting pop-up events, offering exclusive bundles, or encouraging social media engagement with tags and posts.

GROWTH WORK
PLAN YOUR MARKETING MAGIC

Set a timeline for each tactic or activity in your sales strategy. For example, plan a limited-edition clothing drop during Black History Month.

Revisit your financial goals. How much do you need to sell to cover your expenses and make a profit, and by when? For example, $2000 in sales revenue within two months.

GROWTH WORK
STRATEGIC SALES PLANNER CANVA TEMPLATE

Target Market and Customer Segmentation

Target Market	Ideal Customer Profile	Marketing Methods

Sales Strategies and Tactics

Sales Strategy:

Tactics/Activities:

Timeline:

Sales Goals and Targets

Sales Goals Ex. I want to make $1,000	Sales Platform Ex. Website, TikTok & Instagram	Timeline Ex. 2 Months

GROWTH WORK

CREATE YOUR BRAND'S FIRST SOCIAL MEDIA POST

SOCIAL MEDIA POST CANVA TEMPLATE

Post your caption below:

  USE QR CODE FOR ACCESS TO YOUR CANVA ASSIGNMENTS

BOSS UP | CHAPTER 6 | PAGE 123

**EXCERPT FROM TEEN MAGAZINE
SUMMER 2024 EDITION**

Meet Jalesa Illery, The Teen Entrepreneur Behind Beautified Jaaee

By: Mia Mack

Introducing Jalesa Illery, a 17-year-old powerhouse entrepreneur who is making waves in the hair industry with her business, Beautified Jaaee. With a passion for beauty and a commitment to excellence, Jalesa is redefining the standard of hair care for her clients.

Starting her journey with Beautified Jaaee, Jalesa offers a range of services, including weave installs and locs, showcasing variety and dedication to her craft. Despite the varying prices, one thing remains constant: Jalesa's unwavering commitment to providing top-notch service to her clients.

But Jalesa's ambitions don't stop there. This past summer, Jalessa expanded her services and created a program called Beautified Seniors. Through her program, she teaches seniors the art of wig-making. Her program got the attention of Pix 11 News, and Jalessa was featured as an inspiring teen entrepreneur making a difference in her hometown of East Orange, New Jersey.

For Jalesa, Beautified Jaaee is more than just a business; it's a project that started with a simple desire to bring out the natural beauty in every client. Having experienced the impact of lacking confidence herself, Jalesa believes that everyone deserves to feel special and confident in their own skin. "I like to show everyone that I work with that they are beautiful inside and out."

Promoting herself on Instagram has been a key strategy for Jalesa to express her confidence and showcase her talents to a wider audience. With her love for beauty, there's no doubt that Jalesa Illery is destined for success with Beautified Jaaee.

Jalesa pictured with Katie Corrado, anchor from PIX11 News

Despite facing obstacles, such as moving to a new home, Jalesa remains steadfast in her commitment to fulfilling her purpose and others through her brand. Through Beautified Jaaee, she hopes to inspire confidence and self-love in her clients, one hairstyle at a time.

CHAPTER 7
CONTENT CREATION

As you embark on your journey in the digital world, mastering content creation is critical to building your brand, connecting with your audience, and turning your passion into profit. Whether your interests lie in fashion, gaming, beauty, or any other niche, this chapter will walk you through the essential steps to kickstart your content creation journey.

7 CONTENT CREATION

First, it's crucial to define your niche with clarity and purpose. Your niche is your specialized area of focus within the vast digital landscape, and it serves as the cornerstone of your content creation journey. When selecting your niche, it's essential to choose a topic that not only ignites your passion but also aligns with your expertise and interests. Consider what topics or industries you understand deeply and feel enthusiastic about discussing or exploring further. Your niche should reflect your unique talents, experiences, and perspectives.

Student designers showcasing their work at Teen Entrepreneur Pop Up Shop

Additionally, consider the needs and preferences of your target audience. What topics resonate with them? What problems or challenges are they facing that you can help address? By carefully considering these factors, you can ensure that your chosen niche not only aligns with your personal passions but also has the potential to attract and engage your audience effectively.

This thoughtful selection process lays a solid foundation for the content you will create, setting you on the path toward establishing yourself as a credible and influential voice within your chosen niche.

Understanding Your Audience

Understanding your audience is a fundamental aspect of successful content creation. You are not just creating content; you are creating content that resonates deeply with your audience, addresses their needs, and adds value to their lives.

To truly connect with your audience, you need to dive deep into their world and gain a comprehensive understanding of who they are.

Start by researching their demographics to gain insights into their age, gender, location, income level, and other relevant factors. This demographic information provides a foundational understanding of your audience's composition, allowing you to tailor your content to suit their characteristics and preferences.

But demographics only scratch the surface. To create content that truly engages and resonates with your audience, you must dig deeper into their interests, hobbies, and passions. What topics are they passionate about? What are their hobbies and interests outside of your niche?

By understanding what makes your audience tick, you can tailor your content to align with their interests and capture their attention more effectively.

Furthermore, it's essential to identify your audience's pain points and challenges. What problems are they facing in their lives or in relation to your niche? By addressing these pain points through your content, you can position yourself as a trusted authority and provide valuable solutions that resonate with your audience on a personal level.

Rapper Bobby Shmurda promoting teen entrepreneur, Kwan Holmes brand.

To gather these insights, leverage tools like social media analytics, which provide valuable data on your audience's behavior, preferences, and engagement patterns across various platforms. Additionally, consider conducting surveys or polls to directly solicit feedback from your audience and gain deeper insights into their preferences and needs.

Armed with these insights, you can tailor your content strategy to meet your audience's specific needs and preferences, increasing the likelihood of engagement, loyalty, and, ultimately, success in your content creation endeavors.

Choosing the Right Platforms

Once you have a clear understanding of your niche and audience, it's time to choose the right platforms to showcase your content. Whether it's YouTube, Instagram, TikTok, or blogs, select platforms that align with your niche and where your target audience is most active.

Creating High-Quality Content

Creating high-quality content is not just a goal; it's a necessity in today's competitive digital landscape. With so many creators vying for attention, standing out requires a commitment to excellence and a strategic approach to content creation.

Begin by developing a comprehensive content strategy that outlines your objectives, target audience, content themes, and publishing schedule. This strategy serves as a roadmap for your content creation efforts, ensuring consistency, relevance, and alignment with your overall goals.

Consider the type of content that best resonates with your audience, whether it's informative tutorials, entertaining vlogs, inspirational stories, or product reviews. By understanding what content formats and topics resonate with your audience, you can tailor your strategy to maximize engagement and impact.

Investing in quality equipment is another essential component of creating high-quality content. While you don't need the most expensive gear to produce compelling content, having the right tools can significantly enhance the production value of your videos, photos, or other content formats.

Good lighting is everything! First, invest in a quality ring light, which you can purchase on Amazon or at the TikTok shop for a reasonable cost. Additionally, consider investing in a good camera capable of capturing crisp, high-resolution images or video footage. That camera can simply be an iPhone or Android that allows you to record in 4K.

Sound is also super important. A high-quality microphone can ensure clear audio, eliminating background noise and enhancing the overall viewing experience. You can get a microphone that connects to your phone for a reasonable price online.

Content creation will also require good editing tools. Apps such as Cap Cut allow you to polish your content, adding visual effects, transitions, and other enhancements that make your content more engaging and professional-looking. The best part is this app is free.

The most powerful content captures your audience's attention and trust. Therefore, you must prioritize authenticity and storytelling in your content creation process. Authenticity builds trust with your audience and fosters deeper connections, while storytelling creates emotional resonance and keeps viewers engaged.

Share your unique perspective, experiences, and insights authentically, allowing your personality to shine through in your content. Use storytelling techniques such as compelling narratives, relatable anecdotes, and visual storytelling to captivate your audience and keep them coming back for more.

How will you know if your content resonates with your audience? Their likes, comments, and feedback—or lack thereof—will immediately let you know if your audience is locked in. So, it's important to continuously seek feedback from your audience and analyze the performance of your content to identify areas for improvement and refinement. Pay attention to metrics such as engagement rates, audience retention, and feedback from comments and messages. Use this data to iterate on your content strategy, experiment with new formats and topics, and refine your approach to content creation over time.

By developing a strategic content strategy, investing in quality equipment, prioritizing authenticity and storytelling, and continuously refining your approach based on audience feedback, you can create high-quality content that stands out in the crowded digital space and resonates deeply with your audience.

Consistency and Engagement

Consistency is not only a foundational principle of content creation but also a cornerstone of building a loyal and engaged audience. Maintaining a regular posting schedule establishes reliability and trust with your audience, signaling your commitment to delivering valuable content consistently. Consistency breeds familiarity, and as your audience becomes accustomed to seeing new content from you at predictable intervals, they are more likely to return to your platform eagerly anticipating your next post.

Moreover, consistency extends beyond just posting frequency; it also encompasses your content's quality, tone, and messaging. Consistency in these aspects helps reinforce your brand identity and values, creating a cohesive and recognizable presence across all your content channels. Whether it's the aesthetic of your Instagram feed, the voice in your YouTube videos, or the messaging in your blog posts, maintaining consistency fosters a sense of cohesion and unity that resonates with your audience.

In addition to consistency in posting, active engagement with your audience is crucial for encouraging a sense of community and connection. Responding promptly to comments, messages, and mentions demonstrates that you value and appreciate your audience's input, fostering a sense of inclusivity and belonging. By actively engaging with your audience, you create a two-way dialogue beyond mere content consumption, allowing you to build meaningful relationships, gather feedback, and gain insights into your audience's preferences and interests.

Student barbers Dark Blendz shows off barber skills with new clients at Pop Up Explosion

Furthermore, building a community around your content is essential for long-term success as a content creator. A loyal and engaged community not only supports your content but also becomes advocates and ambassadors for your brand, helping to amplify your reach and influence. Encourage interaction and collaboration among your audience members, creating opportunities for them to connect with each other, share their experiences, and contribute to the conversation.

Ultimately, consistency, engagement, and community-building work hand-in-hand to create a positive and impactful content ecosystem.

By staying true to your posting schedule, maintaining consistency in your content, actively engaging with your audience, and fostering a sense of community, you can cultivate a loyal and engaged audience that not only consumes your content but actively participates in and contributes to your success as a content creator.

Collaborating and Networking

Collaborating and networking with other content creators in your niche is a powerful strategy for expanding your reach, growing your audience, and accelerating your entrepreneurial journey.

By forming strategic partnerships and alliances with like-minded creators, you can tap into their audience, leverage their expertise, and unlock new opportunities for growth and collaboration.

One of the most effective ways to collaborate with other content creators is through co-created content. This could involve collaborating on a joint video, podcast episode, blog post, or social media campaign that showcases each other's expertise and content. By combining your talents and resources, you can create content that is more engaging, informative, and valuable to your shared audience while also reaching new audiences through cross-promotion.

Another way to collaborate with fellow content creators is through guest appearances or features. This could involve inviting them to contribute guest posts or interviews on your platform or vice versa. By featuring each other on your respective channels, you can introduce your audiences to new voices, perspectives, and content creators while also gaining exposure to their audience in return.

In addition to direct collaborations, networking with other content creators in your niche is also invaluable for learning, growth, and support. Attend industry events, conferences, and meetups to connect with fellow creators, exchange ideas, and build relationships. Join online communities, forums, and social media groups where you can engage in discussions, share insights, and seek advice from peers who understand the challenges and opportunities of content creation.

Furthermore, don't underestimate the power of mentorship and mentorship networks in your entrepreneurial journey. Seek out more experienced creators who can offer guidance, mentorship, and support as you navigate the ups and downs of content creation and entrepreneurship. Whether through formal mentorship programs, informal mentorship relationships, or mastermind groups, having a supportive network of mentors and peers can provide valuable insights, accountability, and encouragement to help you achieve your goals.

Ultimately, collaborating and networking with other content creators in your niche does more than expand your reach and grow your audience; it helps you build meaningful relationships, share knowledge and resources, and support each other on your entrepreneurial journey. By embracing collaboration, networking, and mentorship, you can accelerate your growth, overcome challenges, and achieve greater success as a content creator and entrepreneur.

Analyzing Performance

Analyzing the performance of your content goes beyond tracking likes, shares, and views. Good analysis allows you to gain actionable insights that drive growth and inform strategic decision-making. By leveraging analytics tools, you can uncover valuable data about your audience's behavior, preferences, and engagement patterns, allowing you to identify what content resonates most with your audience and optimize your strategy accordingly.

Start by tracking key metrics such as engagement rate, audience demographics, and content performance across different platforms. Analyze which types of content perform best, whether it's videos, photos, blog posts, or live streams, and identify common themes or topics that generate high levels of engagement. By understanding what content resonates most with your audience, you can double down on those areas and refine your content strategy to deliver more of what your audience loves.

Additionally, pay attention to audience retention metrics such as watch time, bounce rate, and average session duration. These metrics provide insights into how well your content captures and holds your audience's attention, allowing you to identify opportunities for improvement and refinement.

Furthermore, stay updated with industry trends and algorithm changes to stay ahead of the curve and adapt your strategy accordingly. Social media platforms constantly evolve, and what works today may not work tomorrow. By staying informed about the latest trends, best practices, and algorithm updates, you can ensure that your content remains relevant, discoverable, and engaging to your audience.

Program Director Dr. Jamila T. Davis interviews with news reporters to discuss summer Teen Entrepreneur Pop Up Shops hosted all over the Greater Tristate Area

Monetization Options

As you continue to grow your audience and create engaging content, exploring various monetization options to sustain your entrepreneurial venture is essential. Brand partnerships, affiliate marketing, and sponsored content are excellent ways to monetize your platform and generate revenue while providing value to your audience. Collaborating with brands that align with your niche and values allows you to create authentic, sponsored content that resonates with your audience and enhances your credibility as a trusted influencer.

Additionally, building a loyal audience willing to support you through methods like Patreon or merchandise sales is critical to sustaining your entrepreneurial venture in the long term. Offer exclusive perks, rewards, and behind-the-scenes access to your most dedicated fans through subscription-based platforms like Patreon, or create and sell branded merchandise such as clothing, accessories, or digital products that appeal to your audience's interests and passions.

Ultimately, analyzing the performance of your content, staying updated with industry trends, and exploring various monetization options are essential components of a successful content creator's toolkit.

This is the ad that helped Dr. Jamila T. Davis generate her first million dollars in sales

By leveraging data-driven insights, staying informed about industry developments, and diversifying your revenue streams, you can build a sustainable and thriving entrepreneurial venture that resonates with your audience and delivers long-term value.

User-Generated Content

Harnessing the power of User-Generated Content (UGC) creators can indeed be a game-changer for teen entrepreneurs looking to boost their visibility and credibility in the digital realm.

Let's examine the story of Keisha: a teen entrepreneur who focuses on sustainable fashion.

Keisha, deeply committed to promoting eco-friendly fashion choices, encouraged her followers to share photos of themselves styling her eco-conscious clothing line. By embracing UGC, Keisha not only showcased her products but also fostered a sense of community and belonging around her brand. As her followers shared their personal style journeys with her clothing, Keisha's brand became more than just a collection of garments; it became a movement—a platform for like-minded individuals to connect, inspire, and advocate for sustainable fashion practices.

Reposting this UGC on her Instagram and website, Keisha amplified her brand's reach and impact, leveraging her customers' authentic voices and experiences to attract new followers and customers. This user-generated content was powerful social proof, validating Keisha's brand and building trust with her audience. As a result, Keisha not only saw an increase in sales but also experienced heightened engagement and loyalty from her growing community of followers.

Keisha focused on strategic content creation techniques to further amplify her visibility and reach. She optimized her content for search engines by incorporating relevant keywords and meta tags, ensuring that her brand would rank higher in search results and attract organic traffic. Collaborating with influencers in the sustainable fashion space allowed Keisha to tap into their established audiences and expand her reach to new potential customers.

Keisha also prioritized creating shareable content that resonated with her audience and encouraged them to spread the word. By crafting compelling narratives, showcasing her brand's values, and highlighting the unique features of her products, Keisha created content that inspired her followers to engage, share, and advocate for her brand.

Utilizing hashtags strategically, Keisha increased discoverability and engagement, making it easier for potential customers to find her content and connect with her brand. Cross-promoting her content across multiple platforms further expanded her reach and allowed her to connect with diverse audiences across different channels.

In addition to these strategies, Keisha implemented a content calendar to stay organized and consistent with her posting schedule. By planning and scheduling her content in advance, she ensured a steady stream of engaging content that kept her audience excited and engaged.

Keisha also leveraged tools like Canva and Cap Cut to bring her creative vision to life. With Canva's user-friendly graphic design templates, Keisha created visually stunning social media posts, banners, and promotional materials that captured her brand's aesthetic and ethos. Cap Cut's mobile video editing capabilities allowed Keisha to edit videos with ease, add effects, and produce professional-looking content—all from her smartphone.

By following these steps—harnessing the power of UGC, focusing on strategic content creation, utilizing tools and platforms effectively, and staying true to her passion and authenticity—Keisha embarked on a successful content creation journey as a teen entrepreneur. With dedication, creativity, and perseverance, she turned her entrepreneurial dreams into reality, inspiring others to do the same.

You are no different from Keisha. You are now armed and equipped with the information and tools to create winning content that can increase your business's sales. So what are you waiting for? Let's get into it. It's time to create!

CASE STUDIES

Now that you understand the power of content creation and visual storytelling, let's take a look at two case studies that show how creative content can captivate audiences and boost brand awareness.

Meet Alexis

Alexis, 17, had always loved designing custom sneakers, but she needed a way to share her creations with a broader audience. She decided to use Instagram and TikTok to visually showcase her design process.

Alexis posted time-lapse videos of herself sketching, painting, and customizing sneakers, which quickly caught people's attention. She also created "before and after" shots of old shoes transformed into unique pieces of wearable art. Her TikTok videos, often using trending music, went viral in the sneaker community, earning her thousands of views. On Instagram, she engaged her followers by asking them to vote on design ideas through stories, making her audience feel involved in the process.

The high-quality content and behind-the-scenes glimpses not only grew her follower count but also led to increased sales. Alexis found that storytelling through content allowed her to connect emotionally with her audience, turning her passion into a profitable business.

Meet Jaylen

Jaylen, 18, had always been passionate about fitness and launched a personal training business aimed at helping teens stay active. To stand out, he decided to focus on building a strong online presence using user-generated content.

Jaylen encouraged his clients to share their fitness progress and workouts on Instagram, tagging his account and using the hashtag #TrainWithJaylen. He reposted their stories and achievements, showing how his training was making a difference. To keep his followers engaged, Jaylen also posted workout challenges and fitness tips on TikTok, creating a sense of community around his brand. His clients loved being featured on his page, and their shared posts helped spread the word about his services.

The combination of client testimonials and engaging fitness content led to more followers and new clients. By focusing on authentic content created by his clients, Jaylen quickly gained credibility and grew his personal training business beyond his local area.

In conclusion, both Alexis and Jaylen successfully leveraged content creation to grow their businesses. Alexis used visual storytelling to showcase her custom sneakers, engaging her audience with behind-the-scenes content. Jaylen relied on user-generated content to build a sense of community around his personal training brand, empowering clients to share their progress.

GROWTH WORK
PLAN YOUR MARKETING MAGIC

Ready to unleash your content creation superpowers? Let's turn your passion into impactful content that resonates with your audience and craft a captivating content strategy.

 What types of content will you create, and how often? Develop a roadmap for your content that aligns with your audience's interests and your brand's goals.

 Gear up for success. What tools and equipment do you need to create high-quality content? Invest in essentials like cameras, microphones, and editing software to elevate your content.

GROWTH WORK
PLAN YOUR MARKETING MAGIC

Stay true to yourself. Authenticity is key in the world of social media. How will you infuse your personality and voice into your content to build trust with your audience?

How often do you plan to post to maintain engagement without overwhelming your audience? What's the ideal rhythm for sharing your content across different platforms?

Set specific goals for your social media metrics. Aim for likes, views, comments, and shares. Even though algorithms are unpredictable, these targets help you stay focused and measure your progress.

GROWTH WORK
SHOT LIST CANVA TEMPLATE

Content Shot List

MONTH: _____

Date	Content Type	Details
EX. 4/1/24	EX. Reel - Shirt Styled 3 Ways	EX. Styling Details: Girls Night Out, Chill Vibes, Dressed Up
EX. 4/3/24	EX. Get Ready With Me Girl's Night Out	EX. Style a fun girl's night out look wearing branded t-shirt and miniskirt Include accessories & handbag

NOTES

GROWTH WORK
CONTENT CALENDAR CANVA TEMPLATE
CONTENT CALENDAR SAMPLE

CONTENT CALENDAR
MONTH: April 2024

	1 Useful Tip (How To Style Your Shirt 3 Ways) EXAMPLE	2 Client Review of Product	3 GRWM Rocking My Merch	4 Pack an Order With Me	5 Brand Mission Post	6
7	8 Client Testimonials	9 Let's Design A New Shirt Together	10	11 Spring Collection Preview	12 Get Ready With Me Girl's Night Out	13
14	15 Motivation Monday Quote	16 Spring Fashion Trends We Love	17	18 4 Fashion Rules to Follow	19 Pick Spring Shirts with me	20
21	22 Click to Write Here	23 Click to Write Here	24	25 Click to Write Here	26 Click to Write Here	27
28	29 Click to Write Here	30 Click to Write Here				

USE QR CODE FOR ACCESS TO YOUR CANVA ASSIGNMENTS

BOSS UP | CHAPTER 7 | PAGE 139

**EXCERPT FROM TEEN MAGAZINE
SUMMER 2024 EDITION**

Meet Isaiah Stewart: The Teen Visionary Transforming Financial Literacy in Newark

By Sa'Rai Gordon

Introducing Isaiah Stewart, a 16-year-old trailblazer determined to revolutionize financial literacy in Newark. With a passion for finance and a drive to break the bonds of poverty, Isaiah is already making significant strides toward becoming a financial advisor and eventually opening his own credit union.

Isaiah's journey began at the Federal Credit Union in Cranberry, where he worked as an office manager assistant with his parents. This early exposure to finance has given him a unique insight into the challenges many adults face, even in their later years. "Without financial literacy, you're relatively chasing money forever, which means you're working forever," Isaiah explains, highlighting his commitment to changing this narrative.

Isaiah doesn't just want to serve his local community; he intends to make financial education accessible to thousands of Newark teens and college students. This summer, he is launching a groundbreaking financial literacy pop-up shop with the help of his mother. The goal? To equip young people with the skills they need to achieve financial independence and stability.

Through a series of engaging workshops and practical programs, Isaiah aims to teach the importance of money management, savings, and investments. He believes that by instilling these crucial skills early on, he can help young people build a foundation for lifelong financial success. "I want to provide youth with the mindset, skills, and resources to live their lives smarter and not harder," Isaiah says.

Isaiah's mission is deeply personal. After witnessing the struggles of many adults, including those well into their senior years, he is committed to breaking what he calls a "generational curse" of financial instability. His pop-up shop will serve as a beacon of hope for Newark's youth, offering them the knowledge and tools to navigate the often complex world of finance.

> "I want to provide youth with the mindset, skills, and resources to live their lives smarter and not harder." - Isaiah Stewart

Isaiah's efforts are more than just a business endeavor; they are a movement toward economic empowerment and community upliftment. By targeting teens and young adults, he hopes to create a ripple effect leading to stronger, more financially literate communities.

For Isaiah, empowering individuals and communities to build a better future is more than just a goal—it's a commitment. He envisions a world where financial literacy is not a privilege but a fundamental right accessible to all. Through his innovative pop-up shop, Isaiah is paving the way for a new generation of financially savvy individuals who can break the cycle of poverty and achieve their dreams.

Isaiah Stewart's story is a testament to the power of youth visionaries. As he prepares to launch his financial literacy pop-up shop this summer, he inspires his peers and is a beacon of hope for the future. By equipping Newark's youth with essential financial skills, Isaiah is not only transforming lives but also contributing to the economic resilience of his community.

As we look to the future, it's clear that leaders like Isaiah are crucial in shaping a more equitable and prosperous society. His dedication to financial education and empowerment reminds us that change is possible, and it often starts with a single, determined individual. Keep an eye out for Isaiah Stewart's financial literacy pop-up shop—it's set to make a significant impact on Newark and beyond.

CHAPTER 8
ESTABLISHING YOUR PRESENCE ON THE INTERNET

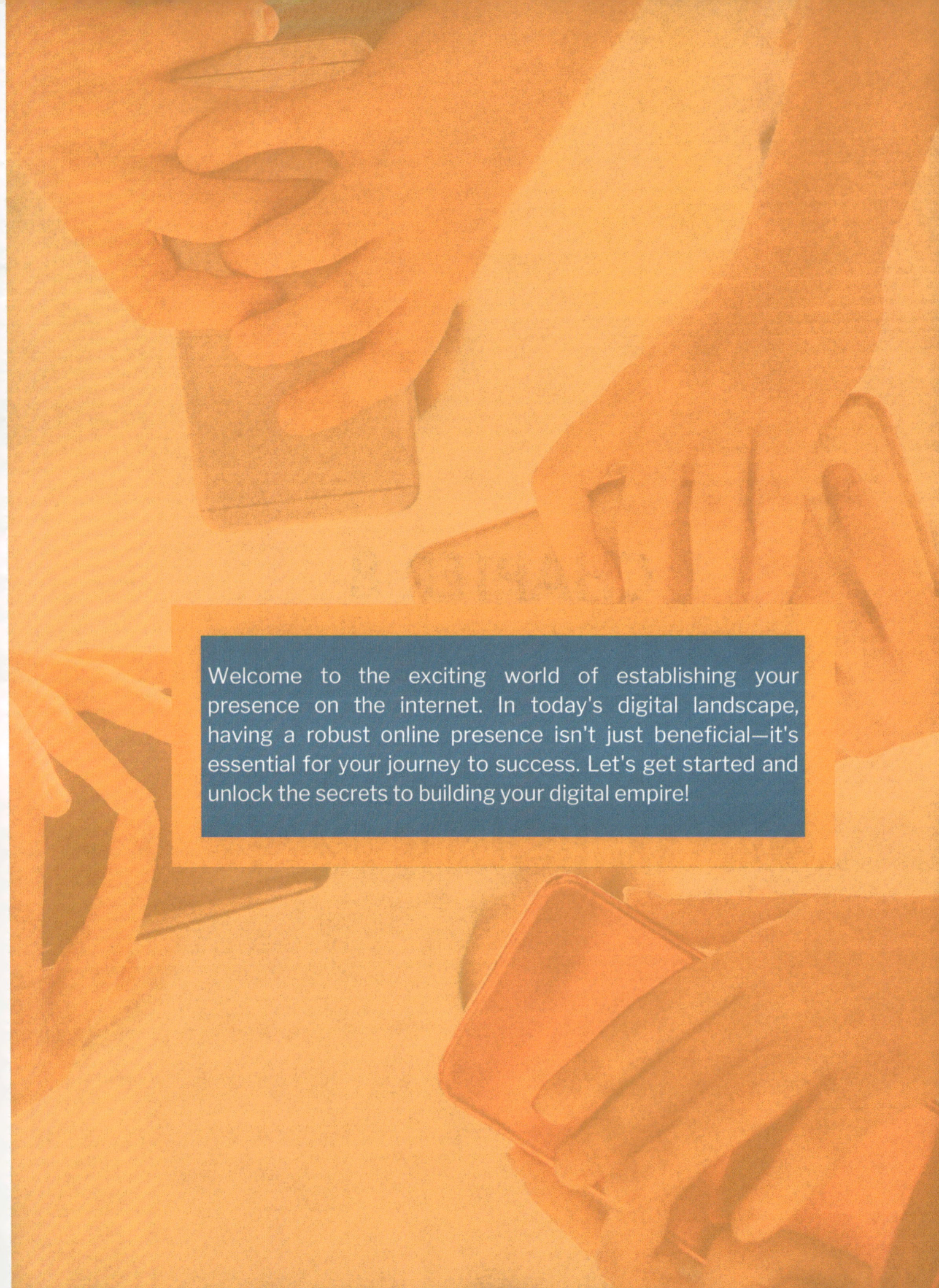

Welcome to the exciting world of establishing your presence on the internet. In today's digital landscape, having a robust online presence isn't just beneficial—it's essential for your journey to success. Let's get started and unlock the secrets to building your digital empire!

8 ESTABLISHING YOUR PRESENCE ON THE INTERNET

Build Your Website

First, let's talk about your online home—your website. Picture it as your digital storefront, the place where potential customers stroll in to get a glimpse of what you offer. It's more than just a website; it's your online resume and portfolio rolled into one. Choose a platform that matches your style and budget.

Design it to mirror your brand identity using colors, fonts, and imagery that resonate with your audience. Showcase your offerings with stunning visuals and compelling descriptions. And don't forget to start a blog; it's your chance to share your expertise and attract visitors like bees to honey. Remember to make it mobile-friendly—because, let's face it, everyone's glued to their smartphones these days!

Choosing the Right Platform:

When considering the right platform for your website, it is critical to explore options that align with your business goals and technical abilities. Let's look at popular choices: Shopify, Wix and WordPress.

Shopify might be your go-to platform if you enter e-commerce and sell products online. It's tailored for online businesses, offering customizable templates, secure payment options, and integrated marketing tools.

With Shopify, you can effortlessly set up your online store, manage inventory, and track sales, all while receiving top-notch customer support.

For those just starting out and seeking a user-friendly approach, **Wix** shines as a beginner-friendly website builder. Its drag-and-drop interface empowers you to craft a customized site without any coding skills.

Wix has diverse templates catering to various industries and design preferences.

It also provides built-in SEO tools, mobile optimization, and analytics, making it a comprehensive solution for website creation.

Powering millions of websites worldwide, **WordPress** offers versatility and scalability. Its robust content management system is excellent for diverse website types, including blogs, portfolios, and e-commerce stores. However, its extensive library of themes and plugins may demand more technical expertise than Wix or Shopify.

Essential Website Content

Creating a website is like setting up your digital storefront—it's where customers will learn about your brand, browse your products or services, and decide whether to engage with your business. Here's a breakdown of the basic elements your website should include to make a strong impression and provide a seamless user experience.

Home Page

First Impressions Matter: Your homepage is the first thing visitors see, so make it count. It should convey who you are and what your business offers. Key elements include:

- **Headline:** A strong, clear headline that captures your brand's essence.
- **Subheadline:** A brief explanation of what you do.
- **Imagery:** High-quality images or videos that represent your brand and instantly capture attention.
- **Call to Action (CTA):** Encourage visitors to take the next step, like "Shop Now" or "Learn More."

Navigation

Guide Your Visitors: Navigation helps users find what they need quickly and easily. Key elements include:

- **Menu Bar:** Clearly labeled menu items that guide users to different sections of your site (e.g., Home, About, Products, Contact).
- **Search Bar** (Optional): A search feature can enhance user experience by allowing visitors to find specific information quickly.
- **Sticky Navigation (Optional):** Consider keeping the navigation bar visible as users scroll down the page for easy access.

About Page

Tell Your Story: This is where you share the background of your business, your mission, and what sets you apart from competitors. Key elements include:

- **Founder's Story:** A personal touch that connects with your audience.
- **Mission Statement:** What drives your business?
- **Imagery:** Include photos of your team, workspace, or anything visually representing your story and mission.
- **Team Introduction (if applicable):** A brief intro to key team members.

Products/Services Page

Showcase What You Offer: Present your products or services with detailed descriptions and high-quality images. Key elements include:

- **Product/Service Descriptions:** Explain what you offer and how it benefits your customers.
- **Pricing Information:** Transparent pricing helps build trust.
- **Imagery:** Use high-quality photos or videos of your products or services to help customers understand your offer.
- **Call to Action (CTA):** Make purchasing or inquiring about your offerings easy for customers.

Contact Page

Make It Easy to Reach You: Provide clear ways for visitors to get in touch. Key elements include:

- **Contact Form:** A simple form for inquiries.
- **Email Address and Phone Number:** Direct contact information.
- **Imagery:** If applicable, include a photo of your storefront, office, or team to make your business feel more approachable.
- **Physical Address (if applicable):** For businesses with a physical location.

Return and Refund/Cancellation Policy

Whether you're offering products or services, having a clear policy that sets expectations for your customers and protects your business is essential. Here's how you can structure your policy:

- **For Products:** Clearly outline your return policy to set customer expectations and build trust:
    - **Simple and Clear:** Ensure your return policy is easily understood and accessible.
    - **Time Frame:** Specify the window in which customers can return products.
    - **Conditions:** Detail the condition products must be in for a return to be accepted (e.g., unopened, with original packaging).

- **For Services:** Outline your refund or cancellation policy to manage client expectations and protect your business.
    - **Refund Terms:** Specify under what conditions a client may request a refund (e.g., within a specific time frame if the service was not delivered as promised).
    - **Cancellation Policy:** Detail how much notice is required for cancellations and whether any fees are associated with late cancellations or no-shows.
    - **Rescheduling Policy**: Provide information on how clients can reschedule appointments or services and any associated conditions or fees.

Privacy Policy and Terms of Use

Protect Your Business and Customers: A Privacy Policy informs customers how their data is used and protected, while the Terms of Use sets rules for using your website. Both are essential for building trust and safeguarding your business.

- **Privacy Policy:**
  - **Data Collection:** Explain what personal information you collect (e.g., email addresses, payment details).
  - **Usage:** Detail how you use the collected data (e.g., for processing orders marketing purposes) and assure customers that you won't sell their information to third parties or spam them.
  - **Security:** Highlight how you protect customer data to ensure it's secure.

- **Terms of Use:**
  - **User Responsibilities:** Outline what users can and cannot do on your website (e.g., not to misuse your content or engage in illegal activities).
  - **Intellectual Property:** Explain that the content on your site, including images and text, is protected by copyright and cannot be used without your permission.
  - **Disclaimers:** Include any disclaimers regarding the accuracy of the information on your site and limit your liability for any issues that may arise from using your site.

> **PRO TIP**
>
> Note: You don't need to be a legal expert to create these policies.
>
> - **Templates:** Platforms like Wix and Shopify offer customizable templates for Return and Refund/Cancellation Policy, Privacy Policy, and Terms of Use. These templates can be easily tailored to fit your specific business needs.
> - **Competitors:** Check out the websites of companies similar to yours to see how they handle these policies. This can provide additional ideas and guidance when crafting your own.

Optional But Recommended Content

While these elements aren't necessary to get your website up and running, they can add extra value and help grow your business.

- **Blog:** A blog is a cool way to share your thoughts, stories, events, and expertise. It can help your audience connect with you and learn more about your work and expertise. One post monthly can make a difference!

- **Email Capture:** Collecting emails lets you stay in touch with your audience and keep them updated on new products, events, or special offers. Add a simple sign-up form on your website. It's an easy way for customers and potential customers to stay connected with you.

Social Media Intergration

Connect Across Platforms: Link your social media accounts to build a consistent online presence. Key elements include:

- **Social Media Buttons:** Allow visitors to easily follow you on other platforms.
- **Embedded Feeds:** Show a live feed of your social media posts.
- **Imagery:** Ensure your social media visuals are consistent with your website's branding.

> **Spoiler Alert: The next page will explore how to effectively use social media to amplify your brand and drive traffic to your site.**

Footer

Wrap It Up Professionally: The footer is the section at the bottom of your website and often contains important links and information. Key elements include:

- **Quick Links:** Include links to key pages like Home, Shop/Book, About, and Contact.
- **Social Media Icons:** Encourage visitors to connect with you on social platforms.
- **Legal Information:** Include links to your return policy, privacy policy, and terms of service.
- **Newsletter Signup (optional):** A form for visitors to subscribe to your email list.
- **Blog (optional):** Add the link to for visitors to check out your blog.

Mobile Optimization

Be Mobile-Friendly: Ensure your website looks great and functions well on smartphones and tablets. Key elements include:

- **Responsive Design:** Your site should automatically adjust to fit different screen sizes.
- **Imagery:** Use images that load quickly and maintain high quality on smaller screens.
- **Test:** If possible, check your site while in draft mode on various devices to see what others will see.

Brand Consistency

Consistency is key to building a strong brand. Refer to your brand guide from Chapter 4 to keep your website's look and feel aligned with your overall brand. Use the colors, fonts, and style guidelines from your brand guide to ensure that your website reflects your brand identity, helping to build recognition and trust with your audience.

Social Media Power

Now that your website is set up as your digital storefront, it's time to extend your reach and engage with your audience where they're already spending their time—on social media. Think of social media as the vibrant, buzzing marketplace that surrounds your storefront, where conversations happen, trends are born, and customers discover what's new.

These platforms aren't just for idle scrolling; they're powerful tools that can amplify your brand's visibility and drive traffic to your website. In fact, research* shows that 49% of consumers use social networks for shopping-related research, and 48% typically discover brands on social media.

 Instagram

- **Who Uses It:** Instagram is most popular with young adults, especially those aged 18-34, but people of all ages widely use it.
- **Why It's Great:** Instagram is a visual-first platform where both high-quality photos and engaging videos reign supreme. Whether it's through Reels, Stories, or stunning photo posts, Instagram allows you to creatively showcase your brand and connect with your audience.
- **How to Use It:** Focus on creating short, engaging videos that tell your brand's story, demonstrate your products, or give a behind-the-scenes look at your business. Reels are particularly effective for reaching new audiences since Instagram's algorithm often favors video content in the explore feed. Additionally, make sure your photos are high-quality and visually appealing—crisp, well-lit images can capture attention and make your brand look more professional.

TikTok

- **Who Uses It:** TikTok is hugely popular with teens and young adults, especially those aged 16-24, making it a go-to platform for reaching a younger, highly engaged audience.
- **Why It's Great:** TikTok is all about short, creative videos that can go viral quickly. It's the perfect platform for showing off your brand's fun and authentic side, with content that's designed to be shared and discovered by a large audience.
- **How to Use It:** Focus on creating short, snappy videos that reflect your brand's personality and catch people's attention within the first few seconds. Participate in trending challenges, use popular music, and include hashtags to help your videos reach a wider audience. Don't be afraid to show the lighter side of your brand—TikTok is all about entertainment, so keep it fun and engaging.

*Source: GWI Social Media Trends, 2024

Twitter (X)

- **Who Uses It:** Twitter, now called X, is widely used by adults aged 18-49, and its focus is on news and real-time updates on what is trending.
- **Why It's Great:** It is like a fast-moving news feed where you can share updates and see what's happening in real-time. It's great for quick communication and staying connected with what's trending in your industry.
- **How to Use It:** Post short, impactful updates highlighting what's new or important in your business. Use hashtags to connect your tweets with more extensive conversations and increase your reach. Engage with others by replying to tweets and retweeting content that aligns with your brand. Keep an eye on trending topics and join in when they are relevant to your business, helping you stay connected with what's current.

YouTube

- **Who Uses It:** YouTube is used by people of all ages, but it's especially popular with those aged 18-49 who are actively seeking out video content to learn, be entertained, or make purchasing decisions.
- **Why It's Great:** YouTube is the go-to platform for all things video. It's perfect for sharing tutorials, product reviews, or any video content that can tell the story of your brand and connect with your audience on a deeper level.
- **How to Use It:** Start a YouTube channel for your business and regularly post videos that either help, entertain, or inform your audience. Focus on clear, engaging titles, detailed descriptions, and relevant tags to make your videos easy to find. Consistency is key—keep posting content to build your subscriber base and keep your audience engaged.

YouTubeShorts

- **Who Uses It:** YouTube Shorts attract a broad audience, particularly those aged 18-34, who love quick and engaging video content that they can consume on the go.
- **Why It's Great:** YouTube Shorts are the perfect way to create quick, attention-grabbing videos. Like TikTok, Shorts are great for delivering bite-sized content that can spark interest in your brand and drive viewers to your longer videos.
- **How to Use It:** Create short, engaging videos that quickly capture attention and highlight your brand or products. Use Shorts to give a preview of your longer content, share quick tips, or showcase exciting moments related to your business. The goal is to keep it snappy and visually appealing to maximize engagement.

Facebook

- **Who Uses It:** Facebook is particularly popular with adults aged 25-54. Targeting these older age groups is crucial because they often have more disposable income and are more likely to make purchasing decisions for themselves and their families.

- **Why It's Great:** Facebook is a powerful tool for building a community and sharing detailed content about your brand. Adults on Facebook often love to see young people working on their businesses, which can help you gain support and build a loyal following.

- **How to Use It:** Once you have a personal profile, set up a Facebook Page for your business. Share posts that provide value to your audience, and join groups relevant to your industry. Leverage your adult family members, who are most likely on thier platform, by encouraging them to share your posts and support your business. Engage with your followers by responding to comments and messages.

Pinterest

- **Who Uses It:** Pinterest is especially popular with women aged 25-54, who use the platform for inspiration and planning. This age group is key to target because they substantially influence household spending decisions and often look for products and ideas that meet their needs.

- **Why It's Great:** Pinterest is a highly visual platform perfect for showcasing products, especially in industries like fashion, beauty (think hair and nails), DIY, and more.

- **How to Use It:** Create visually stunning pins that link to your website, blog, or online store. Organize your content into themed boards to make it easy for users to find what they want.

LinkedIn

- **Who Uses It:** LinkedIn is most popular with professionals aged 25-49. Building relationships with this age group is crucial because they often hold decision-making roles and can open doors to partnerships, mentorships, and business opportunities.

- **Why It's Great:** LinkedIn is the go-to platform for professional networking and is especially valuable for young entrepreneurs looking to connect with industry leaders and potential mentors. Adults on LinkedIn are often impressed by young people who are taking charge of their careers early and are usually willing to offer support, advice, and even business opportunities.

- **How to Use It:** Create a professional LinkedIn profile highlighting your business, skills, and achievements. Share content that demonstrates your knowledge and passion for your industry. Engage with posts from professionals in your field to build connections.

Advanced Strategies

As your business starts to grow, some advanced tools and strategies require an increase in your budget spending but can help you take things to the next level. While we won't dive deep into these now, it's good to know what's out there so you can explore them when the time is right.

- **In-App Shopping:** Instagram and TikTok offer in-app shopping features that allow users to discover and purchase products without leaving the platform. These tools can create an easy customer shopping experience and simplify purchasing. However, with in-app shopping and other platform-specific tools, you have less control over the customer experience than your website.

- **Working with Influencers:** Partnering with the right influencers can significantly boost your brand's visibility and credibility. Through product reviews, tutorials, or creative collaborations, influencers can help you reach a broader audience and build trust with potential customers by creating authentic content that showcases your products or services. However, remember that your brand's reputation is partly in their hands. If the influencer's behavior or content doesn't align with your brand values, it could harm your business.

- **Paid Advertising**: All major social media platforms offer paid advertising options that allow you to target specific audiences, boost your reach, and drive more sales. However, running ads can be expensive, especially in competitive markets, and requires careful budgeting to avoid overspending. So, before you take the plunge, it's essential to know the basics of ads, even if you hire an expert to manage them.

 **Be Cautious:** While social media platforms and advanced tools are powerful, relying too much on them can be risky. Social media algorithms change frequently and can Interfere with a well-intended social strategy and budget.

That's why having your website gives you control and acts as a safety net if something changes on social media. Building and maintaining an email list is essential—it allows you to connect directly with your audience without relying on third-party platforms.

Your website and email list help you maintain consistent branding, manage customer interactions, and protect your business from sudden shifts in social media trends.

Maintaining Digital Wellness

In today's world, social media is a powerful tool for building your brand, connecting with others, and growing your business. But it's also important to remember that constantly being online can sometimes take a toll on your mental and emotional well-being. Digital wellness is all about finding a balance—using social media in a way that benefits you without letting it overwhelm you.

Signs You Might Need a Digital Break

- **Feeling Overwhelmed:** If you start feeling stressed or anxious whenever you check your social media accounts, it might be time to take a step back.
- **Comparing Yourself to Others:** It's easy to get caught up in comparing your life or business to what you see online. Remember, social media often shows the highlight reel, not the full story.
- **Struggling to Stay Present:** If you're always thinking about your next post or how many likes you're getting, it might be pulling you away from enjoying real-life moments.
- **Difficulty Sleeping:** Spending too much time on your phone, especially before bed, can make it harder to get a good night's sleep.

Tips for Maintaining Digital Wellness

- **Set Boundaries:** Decide how much time you want to spend on social media each day and stick to it. Consider using apps that track your screen time or set reminders to take breaks. This ensures you're using your time efficiently without burning out.
- **Curate Your Feed:** Follow accounts that inspire and uplift you. Don't be afraid to unfollow or mute accounts that make you feel stressed or inadequate. This keeps your feed relevant and focused on growth.
- **Practice Mindfulness:** Take time each day to disconnect from your devices and reflect on your business strategies. Whether it's brainstorming new ideas, reading a business book, or practicing a hobby that sparks creativity, find activities that help you relax and recharge, making you more effective in your business.
- **Be Intentional:** Use social media with clear business objectives in mind. Instead of scrolling aimlessly, focus on activities that directly benefit your business, like engaging with your audience, researching market trends, or learning new skills that can enhance your brand.
- **Connect Offline**: Building your business isn't just about online presence. Make time to nurture relationships in real life—whether it's networking with potential partners, meeting with mentors, or simply spending time with friends and family to stay grounded and balanced.

The Marriage of Content and Selling

Content creation is a crucial part of building your brand and connecting with your audience. Ultimately, engaging and relevant content can help you attract followers, establish credibility, and drive sales.

Be sure to include your website link in the bio section of every platform to drive traffic and enhance engagement.

Remember, content creation isn't just about selling products; it's about telling your story, sharing your expertise, and providing value to your audience. Whether through blog posts, social media posts, videos, or podcasts, creating content that resonates with your audience can help you build relationships and foster trust.

So, as you embark on your social selling journey, don't forget the power of content creation. Keep sharing your story, providing value to your audience, and engaging with them authentically. This will not only help you attract customers but also help you build a loyal community around your brand.

Teen Entrepreneur shows off artwork for sale at Teen Entrepreneur Pop Up Shop

CASE STUDIES

Now that you've learned how to build a strong online presence through websites and social media, let's explore two case studies that highlight the importance of having an impactful digital presence.

Meet Aaliyah

Aaliyah, 17, had been selling her digital artwork locally, but she wanted to expand her reach beyond her immediate community. To grow her art business, she decided to build a professional online portfolio.

Aaliyah created a website that showcased her work, including detailed descriptions of her creative process and the inspiration behind each piece. She integrated her Instagram feed into the site, allowing visitors to see her latest posts and easily follow her. Aaliyah also added a shop section where customers could purchase prints and commissions directly from her site.

To drive traffic to her portfolio, she used Instagram and TikTok to share time-lapse videos of her artwork, with links directing followers to her website. The professional online presence not only increased her sales but also led to several freelance opportunities. Aaliyah's website gave her the credibility and reach she needed to connect with customers beyond her local area, taking her art business to the next level.

Meet Elijah

Elijah, 18, loved skateboarding and decided to turn that passion into a business by creating and selling custom-designed skateboards. To expand beyond his local market, Elijah set up an online store using Shopify. He showcased his unique skateboard designs with high-quality photos, detailed descriptions, and customer reviews to build trust.

Elijah also integrated his Instagram feed into the store, allowing followers to easily browse and purchase his products. He used Shopify's features to track inventory, manage orders, and offer secure payment options, making the process smooth for both him and his customers.

To drive traffic, Elijah shared behind-the-scenes content of his design process and skateboarding tips on his blog and social media. Within weeks, he saw an increase in orders, with customers coming from all over the country. Shopify helped Elijah grow his business by providing a professional, easy-to-use platform, turning his passion into a thriving enterprise.

In conclusion, young entrepreneurs like Aaliyah and Elijah have set themselves up for success by mastering the art of building an online presence. They understood the power of creating a professional website to showcase their work, connect with their audience, and grow their brand. With determination, creativity, and a strong digital strategy, they are well on their way to expanding their entrepreneurial journeys and achieving greater success in their fields.

GROWTH WORK

ESTABLISHING YOUR INTERNET PRESENCE WITH A WEBSITE

In today's digital age, having a sleek, functional website is crucial for any budding entrepreneur. Before building your site, choosing a platform that suits your business needs is important. Let's take a closer look at Shopify and Wix.

Start by signing up for the free trials for **Shopify.com** and **Wix.com**

Selling Products and Goods? Shopify Is your best bet.

Selling services? Wix will be great for what you need.

Pricing
- Research and compare the pricing plans offered by each platform.
- Consider the pricing for basic and premium features.
- For eCommerce, factor in the processing fees for each transaction.
- Start with the least expensive monthly subscription plan. You can always upgrade later.

Setup Simulation
- Create a basic version of your website using the platform's tools and templates.
- Check out the theme library and pick a design you like. Customize it with colors, fonts, and your business info.
- Use the drag-and-drop editor to set up your site's layout. Make sure to include essential pages like Home, About, and Contact.
- Try adding features like a store or social media links.
- Preview your site to see how it looks on both desktop and mobile devices.

Your Domain Name
Go to GoDaddy.com and find a domain name that suits your business.
Pick something memorable and easy to spell. Write down your choice below:

Revisit Your Budget
Did you stick to it, or will you need to make adjustments?

GROWTH WORK
SOCIAL MEDIA INTEGRATION WORKSHEET

List the two social media platforms that best align with your business goals. For each platform, briefly explain why you chose it and how it integrates with your website and overall online presence.

1. ☐

☐

2. ☐

☐

List the one social media platform and one advanced strategy you will try out when your business is a little further down the road. Briefly explain why you chose them.

☐ and ☐

☐

EXCERPT FROM TEEN MAGAZINE SUMMER 2024 EDITION

Meet Serena Hazelwood: The Resilient Teen Behind Only the Raw Survive

By Zaniyah Austin

Introducing 19-year-old Serena Hazelwood, the dynamic force behind Only the Raw Survive. Hailing from Newark, New Jersey, her journey of resilience and empowerment is inspiring a generation to embrace their struggles and find strength in adversity. Starting her brand at 17, Serena has gone through tough times and faced criticism from those closest to her. She started her brand as a way to not only find comfort within herself but also help those who struggle through hardships.

Only the Raw Survive represents Serena's personal journey brought to life. According to Serena, her logo, the lion, symbolizes the strongest in the jungle as a lion goes through many setbacks that deter them from their survival but they always come out on top. The lion's bravery, nobility, and courage is why they are the most feared animal and why they got the name, "The King Of The Jungle."

Serena spreads light on the trauma she received over the years that made her act out in certain ways as a coping mechanism. She once said, "People think you are crazy because you cope with things in a different way."

She counteracts the negative stigma of mental health and how it is perceived through her message. You do not need to act a certain way in order to be diagnosed with a mental health disorder. It varies from person to person. One may act in destructive ways while another may try to hide it in happier forms. Everybody's mind is different, so their mental issues can not coincide with anyone else's.

As Serena overcame her battle with depression, she became the lion, similar to the king of the jungle in her own story being driven by her unwavering vision and determination to survive. This can be seen on the day she obtained her LLC as it was a triumph, exemplifying how she proved her doubters wrong.

By incorporating her experiences and message into her designs, Serena creates clothing that resonates with her audience on a personal level. Each piece tells a story of resilience and empowerment, reminding wearers that they are not alone in their struggles.

One valuable lesson she said while developing her brand is, "Everybody who claims that they are your friends is not really your friend." This demonstrates not only her growth as a person, but made her realize that in order for you to be at your happiest in life, you have to let the people that hold you back go. Some friends are only meant to be temporary, so it's okay to leave them behind in order to pursue your goals.

As Serena's business continues to grow, she hopes to inspire others through her brand to embrace the hardships of their journey because even if it might be hard now, it is going to be better in the future. By promoting her experience on social media platforms like Instagram and TikTok, people can feel a personal connection with her and even gain guidance on how to deal with their personal issues. So, embrace your journey with courage and determination, knowing that only the real survive.

Serena is a graduate of the Boss Up Program at Essex County College. She has participated in several pop up shops and has made thousands of dollars in sales. She is a true example of an overcomer and the power of entrepreneurship.

CHAPTER 9
CUSTOMER SERVICE AND BUSINESS ETIQUETTE

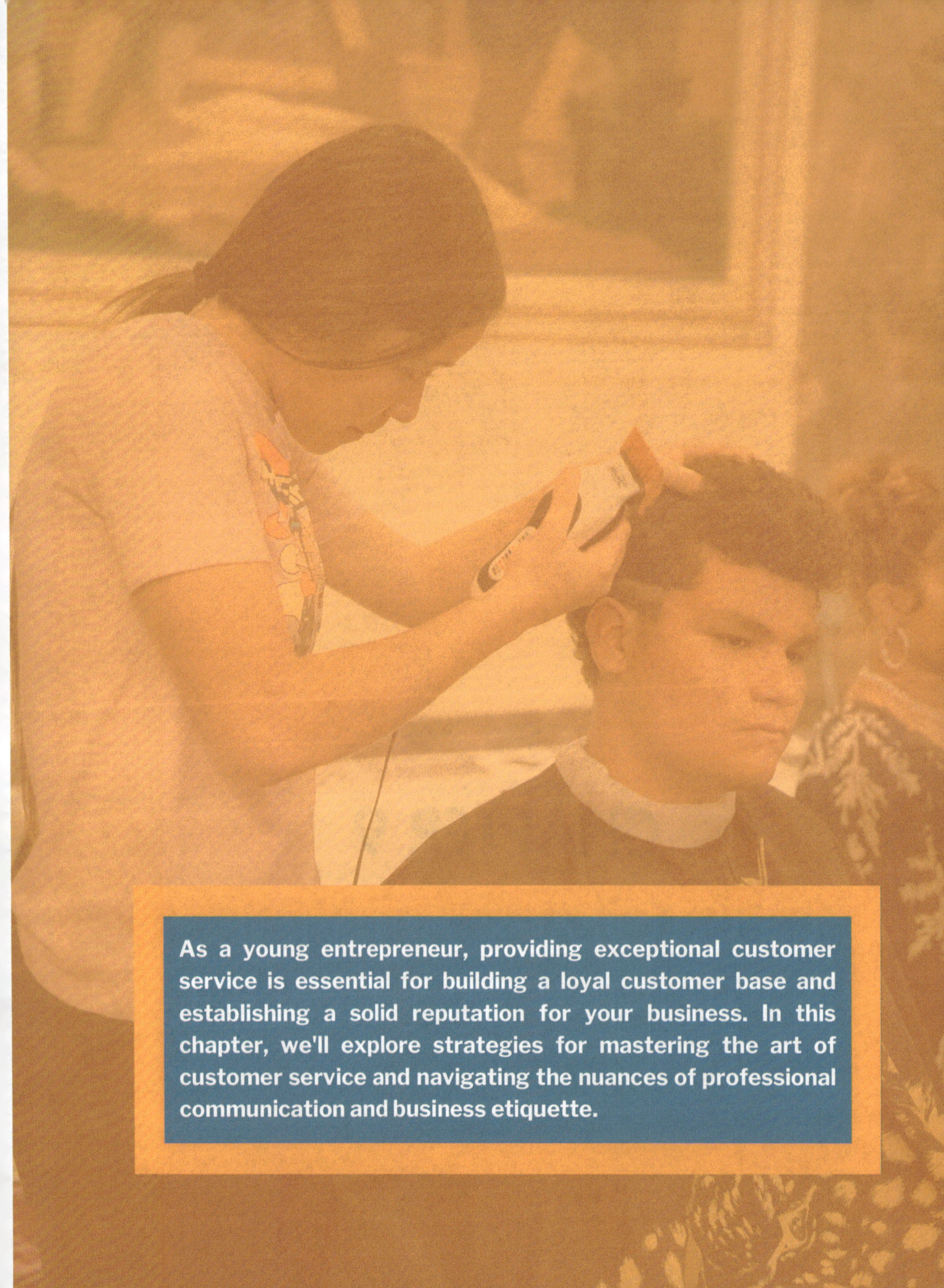

As a young entrepreneur, providing exceptional customer service is essential for building a loyal customer base and establishing a solid reputation for your business. In this chapter, we'll explore strategies for mastering the art of customer service and navigating the nuances of professional communication and business etiquette.

9 CUSTOMER SERVICE AND BUSINESS ETIQUETTE

Navigating Business Etiquette in Different Settings

As a young entrepreneur, you'll interact with various stakeholders, including customers, suppliers, and potential partners. It's essential to conduct yourself professionally in these interactions to build credibility and establish positive relationships.

Mastering the Art of Customer Service: Tips for Creating Happy Customers

- **Listen Attentively:** Whether you're interacting with customers in person, over the phone, or through digital channels, active listening is vital. Pay close attention to their needs, concerns, and preferences. For example, if you run a tutoring service, take notes on the specific subjects or areas where your student is struggling.

- **Personalize the Experience:** Treat each customer as an individual by tailoring your approach to their unique requirements. If you sell handmade jewelry, offer personalized recommendations based on their style preferences or the occasion they're shopping for.

- **Be Prompt and Responsive:** Customers expect quick responses in today's fast-paced world. Whether through email, social media, or text messaging, ensure you have systems in place to promptly reply to inquiries and feedback.

- **Go the Extra Mile:** Surprise and delight your customers by exceeding their expectations. If you run a clothing line, consider including a handwritten thank-you note or a small gift with their order. These small gestures can create a lasting impression.

- **Ask for Feedback and Implement Improvements:** Regularly seek feedback from your customers and use their insights to enhance your products or services. If you offer graphic design services, ask your clients for honest feedback on their experience and areas for improvement.

- **Dress Appropriately:** Whether you're meeting with clients, attending networking events, or pitching to investors, dress appropriately for the occasion. While you don't need to wear a suit, ensure your appearance is neat, well-groomed, and reflects your brand's image.

Mind Your Manners: Basic etiquette goes a long way in business. Always be polite, respectful, and mindful of others' time and personal space. Use phrases like "please," "thank you," and "excuse me" generously.

Listen Actively: When communicating with others, practice active listening. Pay attention to what they're saying, maintain eye contact, and avoid interrupting. Ask thoughtful questions to clarify your understanding and demonstrate your engagement.

Use Professional Language: While it's essential to be yourself, avoid using slang, jargon, or unprofessional language in business settings. Communicate clearly and concisely, using appropriate language for the situation.

Respect Cultural Differences: As an entrepreneur, you may interact with people from diverse backgrounds. Be mindful of cultural differences in communication styles, personal space, and customs. If you're unsure about certain practices, research or ask respectful questions to avoid unintentional offenses.

Resolving Customer Issues with Grace and Efficiency
Even with the best intentions, issues may arise with customers. How you handle these situations can make or break your business reputation.

Acknowledge the Issue: When a customer raises a concern or complaint, address it promptly. Apologize sincerely, even if the issue wasn't directly caused by your business. This shows empathy and a willingness to resolve the problem.

Communicate Transparently: Keep the customer informed throughout the resolution process. Provide regular updates, even if there's no immediate solution. Transparency builds trust and prevents frustration from escalating.

Offer Solutions: Present viable options to address the customer's concerns. If you run an online store and an item was damaged during shipping, offer a replacement or refund. Be willing to compromise and find a resolution that satisfies both parties.

Follow Up: After resolving the issue, follow up with the customer to ensure their satisfaction. Ask for feedback on how the situation was handled and if there's anything else you can do to improve their experience.

Learn and Improve: Use customer feedback and issues as opportunities for growth. Identify areas for improvement in your products, services, or processes, and implement changes to prevent similar issues from occurring in the future.

Mastering customer service, professional communication, and issue resolution will create a positive customer experience and establish a strong foundation for your business's long-term success. Building a loyal customer base and maintaining a professional reputation is essential for any young entrepreneur striving for greatness.

CASE STUDIES

Now, let's dive into some real-world examples with case studies to see these principles in action!

Case Study #1: Delicious Delights Catering - Jacob's Personalized Meal Planning

For Jacob, the teenage entrepreneur behind Delicious Delights Catering, personalized service was the secret ingredient to his success. He understood that every client has unique tastes, dietary needs, and event visions.

One client, the Johnsons, had hired Jacob to cater their son's high school graduation party. Jacob sat down with the family, listening intently as they described their son's favorite dishes, the cultural traditions they wanted to incorporate, and the specific dietary restrictions of some guests.

With this invaluable feedback, Jacob crafted a personalized menu that seamlessly blended flavors and dishes from different cultures while accommodating all dietary needs. He even included a dessert station featuring the graduate's favorite treats.

On the day of the graduation party, the Johnsons were impressed by the exceptional service and attention to detail provided by Jacob and his team. The food was not only delicious but also a true reflection of their family's diverse backgrounds and their son's personal tastes.

The Johnsons couldn't stop raving about Delicious Delights Catering to their friends and family, quickly becoming loyal customers and ambassadors for Jacob's business.

Jacob's Conclusion:

Jacob's personalized approach to catering made the Johnsons' graduation party a memorable success. By listening closely to their needs and creating a custom menu that honored their cultural traditions and dietary restrictions, he delivered exceptional service and delicious food. This attention to detail turned the Johnsons into loyal customers and enthusiastic advocates, showcasing the power of personalized service in building a strong client base and a thriving business.

CASE STUDIES

Case Study #2: Glamour Goddess Designs - Keisha's Professional Communication

Professional communication was key to securing high-profile clients for Keisha, the visionary behind Glamour Goddess Designs, a company specializing in prom, homecoming, and graduation gowns. During a chance encounter at a bridal expo, Keisha struck up a conversation with the mother of a popular high school influencer known for her impeccable style.

Keisha listened intently as the mother described her daughter's desire for a one-of-a-kind prom gown that would turn heads and make a statement on social media. With poise and articulation, Keisha presented her brand's vision and her team's meticulous attention to detail in crafting couture pieces.

Throughout the conversation, Keisha maintained a professional demeanor, having dressed impeccably for the occasion and using language befitting the high-fashion industry. She asked thoughtful questions, demonstrating her genuine interest in understanding the influencer's vision and preferences.

The mother was captivated by Keisha's approach and the passion she exuded for her craft. She saw in Keisha a kindred spirit, someone who understood the importance of exclusivity and could deliver a jaw-dropping gown that would make her daughter the center of attention.

Thanks to Keisha's professional communication skills and ability to connect with the mother on a deeper level, Glamour Goddess Designs secured a lucrative commission to design a custom prom gown for one of the most popular influencers in the region.

Keisha's Conclusion:

Keisha's professional communication and genuine interest in her clients' needs secured a high-profile commission for Glamour Goddess Designs. By listening intently, presenting her brand with poise, and demonstrating a passion for her craft, Keisha connected deeply with the client. This approach not only won the commission but also showcased the importance of professional communication in building client trust and securing business opportunities. Effective issue resolution can enhance a brand's reputation and customer loyalty.

CASE STUDIES

Case Study #3: Amari's Jewels - Efficient Issue Resolution Saves a Prom Night

For Amari, the talented jewelry designer behind Amari's Jewels, efficient issue resolution was essential in maintaining client trust and building a reputation for excellence. One particular client, a high school senior named Samantha, encountered a crisis when the custom necklace she had ordered for her prom night was accidentally damaged in transit.

Panicked and heartbroken, Samantha reached out to Amari, who promptly acknowledged the issue and assured her that the team was working tirelessly to resolve the problem. Amari kept Samantha informed every step of the way, providing regular updates on the progress and the steps being taken to recreate the intricate necklace design.

Within forty-eight hours, Amari and her team had not only resolved the issue but also hand-delivered the recreated necklace to Samantha's doorstep, ensuring it arrived in time for her prom night. They worked around the clock to ensure the piece was flawlessly crafted, capturing every intricate detail of the original design.

Samantha was overwhelmed with gratitude for Amari's commitment to transparent communication and her team's swift resolution of the issue. She was impressed by Amari's Jewels's professionalism, efficiency, and dedication to ensuring their clients' complete satisfaction.

The seamless handling of the crisis strengthened the bond between Amari's Jewels and Samantha, solidifying their reputation as a reliable and trustworthy jewelry designer. Samantha became a vocal advocate for Amari's business, referring her to friends and sharing her positive experience across her social media platforms.

Amari's Conclusion:

Amari's quick and efficient handling of Samantha's crisis not only saved prom night but also solidified Amari's Jewels' reputation for exceptional customer service. By maintaining transparent communication and delivering a flawless replacement in record time, Amari turned a challenge into an opportunity, strengthening customer relationships and boosting business growth. Samantha became a loyal advocate, demonstrating how effective issue resolution can enhance a brand's reputation and customer loyalty.

GROWTH WORK
WHAT WOULD YOU DO? SCENARIOS

In this activity, you'll test your customer service, business etiquette, and problem-solving skills through real-world scenarios, sharpening your abilities, enhancing your professional conduct, and preparing to navigate situations with confidence and grace.

Scenario 1: The Dissatisfied Client

You recently launched your new jewelry line and made your first online sale to a customer named Samantha. A few days later, you received an email from her expressing frustration with the quality of the necklace she purchased. Samantha states that the clasp is flimsy, and one of the gemstones has already fallen out. She demands a full refund and seems quite upset with her experience.

Scenario 2: Making a Great First Impression

You've been invited to attend a local entrepreneurship networking mixer hosted by your city's chamber of commerce. As a young entrepreneur, you're excited about the opportunity to connect with potential mentors, collaborators, and even prospective clients. During the event, you overhear a group discussing the challenges of marketing handmade products online, which happens to be your area of expertise.

GROWTH WORK
WHAT WOULD YOU DO? SCENARIOS

Scenario 3: Addressing Negative Feedback Online

Your new clothing line has been gaining traction on social media, with a growing following on Instagram. However, you recently received a scathing comment from a customer who was unsatisfied with the quality of one of your t-shirt designs. They claim the fabric feels cheap, and the print started peeling after just a few washes. Their negative comment is visible to all your followers.

Scenario 4: Shipping Mishap

You run a successful online bakery specializing in custom cakes and desserts. One of your regular customers, Emily, placed an order for a special occasion cake to be delivered on Saturday for her daughter's birthday party. On Friday evening, your delivery driver informs you that the cake may not arrive until Sunday or Monday, well after Emily's event, because of a vehicle issue.

BOSS UP | CHAPTER 9 | PAGE 171

GROWTH WORK
WHAT WOULD YOU DO? SCENARIOS

Scenario 5: Welcoming Diverse Clients

You're opening a new barber/beauty salon in a neighborhood with a large potential customer base, many of whom speak English as a second language. You're excited about the opportunity to serve a diverse community, but you're also aware of the communication challenges that may arise. How will you address these language barriers to ensure clear communication and great customer service?

Teen Entrepreneur Shane Green pictured during an interviewed with News 12 reporter about his business

**EXCERPT FROM TEEN MAGAZINE
SUMMER 2024 EDITION**

Spotlight on Siyah:
A Young Entrepreneur's Journey

By Mia Mack

Asiyah Williams, a bright and ambitious student at Donald M. Payne Sr. School of Technology, has turned her passion for photography into a thriving business. At 17, Asiyah released "Shots by Siyah," a photography venture that brought out her unique talent for capturing life's most precious moments. She started her journey with the 10-week Boss Up program, which ignited her working spirit and provided the foundation to elevate her hobby into a professional business. "I always loved taking pictures, but this program taught me how to turn that love into something real and sustainable," Asiyah shared.

Networking played a role in Asiyah's success. She leveraged her connections with family and friends, who became not only her first clients but also her biggest advocates. "My family and friends spread the word about my services, and soon enough, I was getting referrals from people I didn't even know." Asiyah's determination didn't stop there; she took to the streets, canvassing local neighborhoods with flyers.

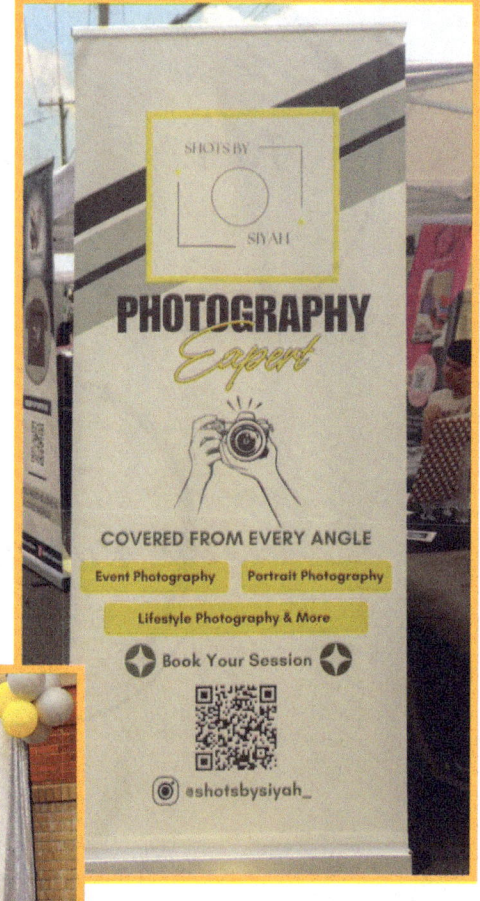

These efforts paid off, helping her to build a loyal customer base and expand her reach. Now, Asiyah dreams of turning "Shots by Siyah" into a lifelong career. Her dedication to her craft and her spirit are evident in every photograph she takes. "Photography is more than just a job for me; it's a way to tell stories and capture memories that people can cherish forever," she said passionately.

Asiyah's story is a testament to the power of hard work, community support, and the courage to pursue one's dreams. With a bright future ahead, she continues to inspire others with her journey and the beautiful images she creates.

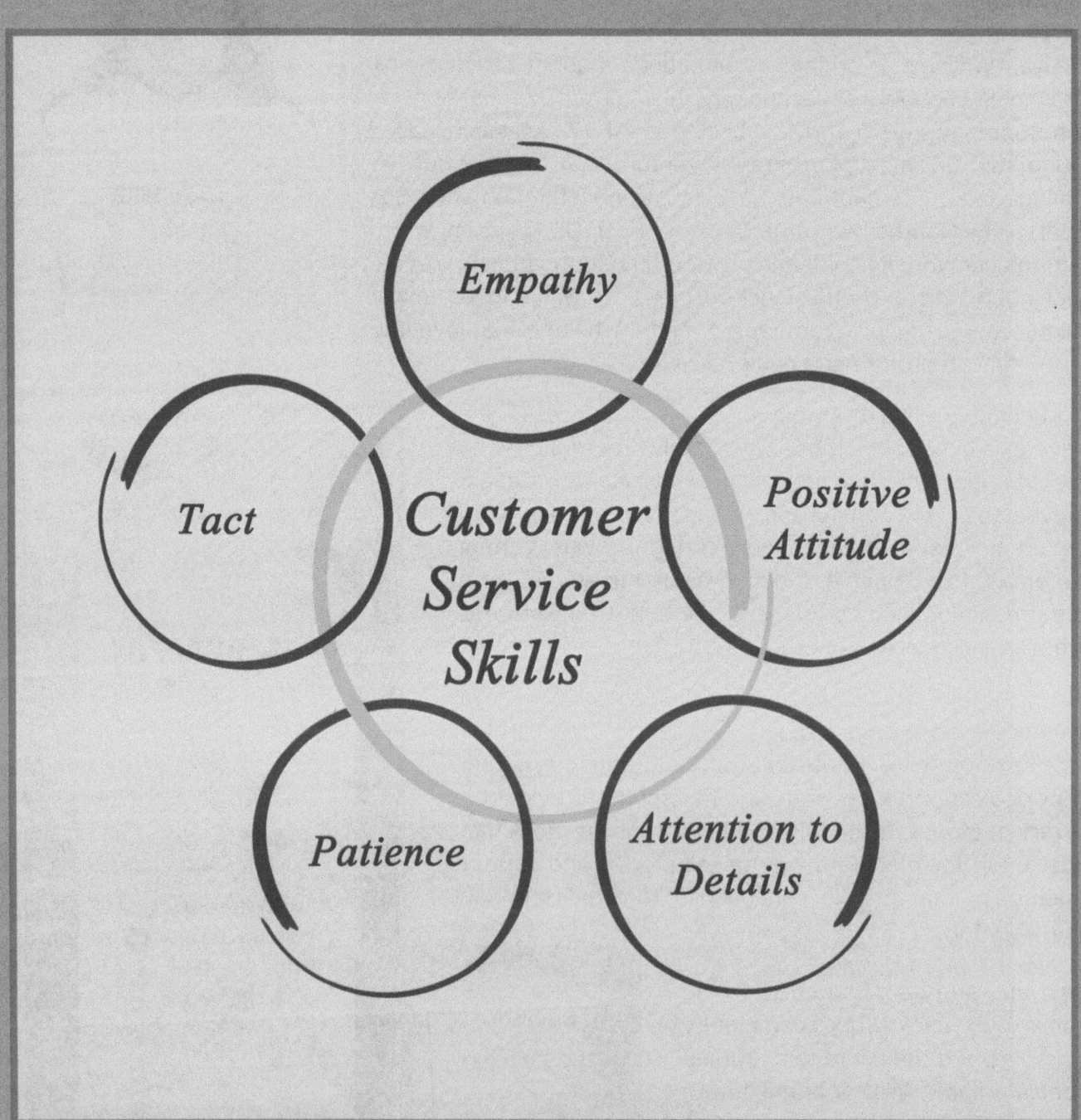

CHAPTER 10
PRODUCING YOUR POP-UP SHOP
TAKE YOUR PRODUCTS TO MARKET

As a young entrepreneur, hosting a pop-up shop is an exciting way to showcase your products or services, connect with customers, and build brand awareness. In this chapter, we'll learn how to plan, set up, and execute a successful pop-up shop. You'll learn strategies for creating a memorable experience, managing logistics, and making sure your pop-up shop runs smoothly from start to finish.

10 PRODUCING YOUR POP-UP SHOP

You've built your brand, created amazing products, and connected with your target audience. Now, it's time to put all that into action and bring your product or services to market with a **pop-up shop**—a temporary retail space where you can showcase your business, meet your customers face-to-face, and make sales. Think of it as your brand's spotlight moment.

In this chapter, we'll explore everything from planning and preparing for your pop-up to engaging your customers on the day of the event and reviewing your success afterward. Whether it's your first or tenth pop-up, the key is to be prepared, stay focused, and enjoy the experience of bringing your business to life in person.

What Is a Pop-Up Shop?

A pop-up shop is a temporary, short-term retail event that allows you to physically set up a store in a specific location for a limited time. It's a great way for small businesses and entrepreneurs to engage with their customers in person, test new products, build buzz, and make direct sales without the long-term commitment of a traditional storefront. Pop-up shops are often used for product launches, seasonal sales, or to create a special shopping experience.

Pop-up shops can take place in a variety of locations—think local markets, malls, festivals, or even shared spaces with other businesses. The goal is to bring your brand into the physical world and make an impression on your customers by offering a unique, personal experience.

Why It Matters

As a teen entrepreneur, a pop-up shop gives you the opportunity to connect with your audience, gain valuable feedback, and generate excitement around your brand. It's also a great way to test the waters before investing in a larger retail presence.

Student bakers anticipate meeting new customers at Teen Entrepreneur Pop Up Shop

Flexibility and Creativity:

One of the greatest advantages of a pop-up shop is its flexibility. You can tailor your space, layout, and even the products or services you offer to fit the needs of each event. Whether you're testing a new idea or bringing a seasonal theme to life, a pop-up allows you to get creative and experiment with different ways to engage your audience. The limited-time nature creates urgency, which can drive excitement and encourage more immediate customer action.

Product-Based Pop-Up Shop

Whether you're selling clothing, accessories, home goods, or artwork, your pop-up shop setup should be visually appealing and organized to attract customers and make browsing easy.

- **Tables and Display Stands:** Use a combination of tables and stands to display your products. Neatly organize your items by type, color, or size. For example, if you're selling various products like accessories or home goods, group similar items together. Use tiered display stands to create height and draw attention to key products.

- **Racks or Shelves (if applicable):** If your products are best displayed hanging (like clothing or bags), set up a clothing rack or shelving unit where customers can easily browse through items. Make sure the products are well-spaced and visible.

- **Mannequins or Product Display Stands:** If you sell wearable items like clothes, jewelry, or even bags, consider using mannequins, display busts, or product stands to showcase how the items look when worn or used. This helps customers visualize the product in action.

Students showcase their faith-based apparel at Teen Pop Up Explosion

- **Signage**: Hang a banner behind your booth or display area with your business name and logo. Use smaller signs to highlight important information like prices, discounts (e.g., "Buy 2, Get 1 Free"), or special product features. Clear, professional signage helps customers quickly understand what you're offering.

- **Packaging and Product Organization:** Display your products neatly in stacks, rows, or sections based on type. If you offer gift packaging or eco-friendly wrapping, make it visible as part of the shopping experience.

- **Interactive Elements (if applicable):** To engage customers, consider offering a small interactive station, like a customization area or product demo. This could be something as simple as letting customers personalize an item or providing samples if appropriate.

- **Comfort and Convenience:** Create a welcoming space by ensuring that customers can easily move around your booth. Provide a small area with a mirror (if necessary for your product type) or have a designated place for customers to ask questions or try products.

Teen entrepreneur demonstrates henna design services on potential new client

Service-Based Pop-Up Shop

Whether you're offering personal services like consultations, fitness training, or creative workshops, your pop-up should create a space that engages potential clients and showcases your expertise.

- **Service Demonstration Area:** Set up a small space where you can offer a demo or sample of your service. For example, if you're offering consultations, create a seating area with a table where you can speak one-on-one with clients. If it's a fitness or creative service, set up a mini demo area for customers to experience your offering directly.
- **Informational Display:** Have a well-organized table with brochures, flyers, or other informational materials about your services. Include details about what you offer, pricing, special promotions, and how clients can book future services.

Student shows off signage with interactive elements for sign ups

- **Sign-Up Options (Digital or Paper):** Provide both digital and paper options for customers to sign up for your services.
  - **Digital Option:** Use a tablet or laptop where customers can input their contact information or book a service on the spot. You can also use a QR code that directs customers to your website or booking page.
  - **Paper Option:** Provide a sign-up sheet where customers can write their name, email, and phone number. Offer pens and make it easy for them to fill out on the go.
- **Interactive Elements (if applicable):** Create an engaging experience for visitors. For example, if you offer personal training, provide short fitness assessments. If you provide creative services, let customers participate in a quick mini-lesson or demo to experience your expertise firsthand.
- **Signage and Branding:** Use a banner with your business name, logo, and a short description of your services. Include signage with details about what you're offering at the pop-up, your website, and any promotions or special offers.
- **Comfortable Seating:** If your service involves consultations or discussions, provide a comfortable seating area with chairs and a small table. This encourages customers to relax and engage in deeper conversations about your offerings.

Example of Teen Entrepreneur signage and branding with business logo, and description

Steps to A Successful Pop-Up Shop

Now that you understand the difference between service-based and product-based pop-ups, let's dive into the steps you'll need to follow to plan and execute your event successfully.

Step 1: Planning and Preparation

Every great event starts with a plan, and your pop-up shop is no different. This is your moment to shine, so setting clear goals is essential.

- **Goal Setting:** What do you want to achieve with this pop-up? If you're selling products, are you aiming to make direct sales or showcase a new collection? If you're offering a service, are you looking to gain new clients or book future appointments? Your goals will guide everything from how you set up your space to how you interact with visitors.

- **Location, Location, Location:** Choosing the right location can make or break your pop-up. For product-based businesses, consider places with high foot traffic, like markets or shopping centers. For service-based pop-ups, think about places where people are likely to engage with you, like festivals, salons, or collaborative spaces.

- **Permits & Licenses:** Don't forget the boring (but essential) stuff! Make sure you have any permits, licenses, or legal requirements in place to sell your products or offer your services at the event.

Estimating Product Inventory (Product-Based)

One of the trickiest parts of preparing for a product-based pop-up shop is knowing how much product to bring. Here's how you can approach this challenge:

Teen entrepreneurs sorting through inventory of products they want to sell at the Teen Pop Up Shop

- **Start Small:** Consider bringing fewer units of each product but offering a wider range. This way, you can gauge what customers are most interested in without overcommitting to large quantities of any one item.

- **Consider Price Points:** Higher-priced items might sell less frequently. More affordable products could move quickly. Factor this in when deciding how much to bring for each product.

- **Pre-Sales or Orders:** Take pre-orders for products you've run out of. Be prepared with a sign-up sheet or an online system so customers can place orders and receive the product later. This keeps the sales momentum going.

- **Create Urgency:** When you start running low on stock, use that to your advantage. Let customers know that products are almost gone, which can create urgency and encourage those who are on the fence to buy before you sell out.

Step 2: Creating the Experience

When it comes to your pop-up, first impressions are everything. Whether you're offering products or services, you want your setup to scream, "This is who I am!" and grab people's attention.

- **Branding & Visuals:** From your color scheme to your signage, everything should reflect your brand. Whether it's a sleek, minimalist design or a bright, bold aesthetic, your pop-up should feel like a physical version of your online presence.
- **Product Display (Product-Based Pop-Ups):** Make your products the star of the show. Use creative displays to catch people's eyes and make it easy for them to interact with your merchandise. Think of ways to make your setup inviting and engaging.
- **Service Demo or Setup (Service-Based Pop-Ups):** If you're offering a service, consider offering free or discounted mini-sessions, consultations, or workshops to showcase your expertise. Make it easy for visitors to experience your service firsthand.
- **Interactive Engagement:** Want to make your pop-up memorable? Offer something extra—whether it's a giveaway, a special discount, or even a quick game. The more interactive, the better. Get people talking about your brand long after they leave.

Step 3: Budgeting and Sourcing

Planning your budget is crucial to keeping your pop-up on track and profitable. Whether you're offering products or services, be clear on your spending so you don't blow through your profits before opening your doors.

- **Budget:** Break down your costs—renting the space, creating your displays, producing extra inventory (for products), or preparing service materials. Don't forget about marketing and any staff you might need to help.
- **Sourcing (Product-Based):** Ensure you've got everything in place, from product stock to your payment system (cash, credit, or mobile payments). You'll also need any displays, signs, or technology like card readers and backup supplies—because things happen.

Student Makeup Artist displaying tools needed for her serviced-based business

- **Sourcing (Service-Based):** For services, think about the tools or supplies you'll need (e.g., styling tools, consultation materials, or digital presentation equipment).

PRO TIP

Remember: Always plan for unexpected costs. Better to be over-prepared than scrambling at the last minute!

Step 4: Marketing and Promotion

You've got your pop-up ready to go—now you need people to show up! Effective marketing is key to getting the word out and building excitement, no matter if you're selling products or offering services.

- **Digital Marketing Strategy:** Social media is your best friend here. Create countdowns, teasers, and engaging posts that get people excited. Use Instagram stories, TikTok challenges, and Facebook events to generate buzz.

- **Website Integration:** Your website is an important part of your digital presence. Use it as a hub for your pop-up event details, showcasing the products or services you'll offer. Include a specific landing page or event announcement on your homepage with relevant info like date, location, and any exclusive offers.

Teen Entrepreneurs snap a behind the scenes pic between breaks of their content shoot for their digital marketing strategy

Teen Entrepreneur talking to the community about his family's new Caribbean cuisine restaurant

- **Link it everywhere:** Add your website link to all your social media posts, invitations, and flyers. Encourage people to visit your site before the event to learn more and even make pre-orders or book services.

- **Offline Promotion:** Don't underestimate the power of old-school marketing. Hand out flyers, put up posters, and tap into your community for word-of-mouth promotion. Collaborate with local businesses or influencers to spread the word.

- **Invitations:** Make a VIP list! Whether it's influencers, local media, or friends and family, personal invitations can create a sense of exclusivity and excitement.

Wrapping Up: Your Pop-Up Shop Success

After the dust settles and the doors close, it's time to review how things went.

- **Sales & Goals Assessment (Product-Based):** Look at your numbers—how much did you sell? Did you meet your goals? Reflect on what worked and what didn't.
- **Client Engagement Review (Service-Based):** Did you gain new clients or make future appointments? Were there any common themes in customer feedback?
- **Next Steps:** Take what you've learned and plan your next move. Whether it's another pop-up or growing your business online, the experience you've gained is invaluable.

Final Thought:

Running a pop-up shop is more than just selling your products or services—it's about building relationships, testing new ideas, and bringing your brand to life. Each pop-up event is an opportunity to learn, grow, and make an impact on your community.

Remember, even if things don't go perfectly, you're gaining valuable experience that will shape you as an entrepreneur. Stay flexible, have fun, and trust the process—you've got this! Now that you've mastered the basics of creating a pop-up shop, it's time to put your plans into action and watch your hard work pay off.

GROWTH WORK

POP UP SHOP PREP

Your Go-To-Market Strategy

Setting Your Goals: What's your main goal for this pop-up? (*Example: Make a $100 profit, get 20 potential customer emails, and promote the brand.*)

What Will You Sell? List the products or services you'll offer:

What Are Your Expenses? For example: materials, advertising, venue.

Pricing for Profit: How much will you charge, and how many sales will you need to achieve in order to make the "Big Flip" and make a profit?

GROWTH WORK
POP UP SHOP PREP

This worksheet will help you plan out the essential branding elements for your pop-up. Once completed, you'll transfer this information to Canva to create your banner, pricing sheet, and business cards. Remember to use your brand guide.

Stand-Up Banner

A **stand-up banner** is a large, vertical sign to promote your business at events or pop-ups. The banner is easy to set up, stands on its own, and grabs attention from a distance.

Typical Dimensions:
- Width: 33 inches (around 2.75 feet)
- Height: 78 inches (around 6.5 feet)

Make sure your banner is clear and easy to read, with your most important information prominently displayed:

- **Business Name**
- **Business Logo**
- **Photos of Product or Service**
- **Key Message** *(What's the main thing you want people to know? Example: Affordable, handmade jewelry!)*
- **Phone, Website, and Social media**

Create your Stand-Up Banner using the Canva template.

  USE QR CODE FOR ACCESS TO YOUR CANVA ASSIGNMENTS

PRO TIP

Use the Canva QR code app to easily generate a QR code that links to your website or social media. This makes it quick and easy for customers to connect with you digitally.

BOSS UP | CHAPTER 10 | PAGE 185

GROWTH WORK
POP UP SHOP PREP

Business Cards

A **business card i**s a small, powerful tool for making a lasting impression on potential customers and partners.

At events or pop-ups, a business card allows people to remember your business and reach out to you later quickly. It's a convenient way to share your contact information and reinforce your brand identity.

Typical Dimensions: 3.5 x 2 inches (standard business card size)

Include your most important information:

- **Your Name**
- **Your Title** (Example: CEO, Owner, or Founder)
- **Business Logo**
- **Contact Information** (phone, email, website)

Create your Business Card using the Canva template.

USE QR CODE FOR ACCESS TO YOUR CANVA ASSIGNMENTS

PRO TIP

Make sure the card is easy to read with a clean layout, and avoid cluttering it with too much information. Choose a high-quality finish like matte or gloss paper to make your card feel professional and ensure it stands out.

GROWTH WORK
POP UP SHOP PREP

Pricing Sheet

A pricing sheet is a single-page document used to showcase your business at events or pop-ups. This will provide your customers with an overview of your products or services and the prices.

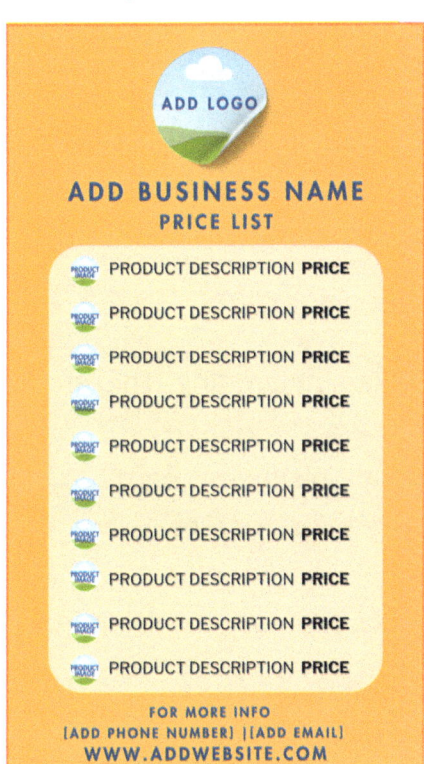

Typical Dimensions: 8.5 x 11 inches (standard paper size)

Include your most important information:

- Business Name
- Business Logo
- Each product or service should have:
    - A brief description
    - A photo
    - Pricing
- Phone number, website, and social media handles or QR code

Create your Pricing Sheet using the Canva template.

  USE QR CODE FOR ACCESS TO YOUR CANVA ASSIGNMENTS

PRO TIP

Make sure the prices are easy to find by using bold fonts for the prices. Use quality photos and keep the product descriptions short and simple.

BOSS UP | CHAPTER 10 | PAGE 187

GROWTH WORK
POP UP SHOP PREP

Download Your Sales Materials

Now that you've designed your banner, business cards, and pricing sheet, it's time to download and print them. Follow these steps to ensure that everything looks professional and is ready in time for your pop-up!

Downloading Your Designs from Canva

- **Go to your Design in Canva:** Open Canva and navigate to the designs you created for your banner, business cards, and pricing sheet
- Click on the Share Button: In the top-right corner, you'll see a 'Share' button. Click on it to open the download options.
- **Choose the File Type:**
    - Banners and Pricing Sheets: Choose 'PDF Print' for high-quality printing. This ensures your designs look crisp and professional.
    - Business Cards: Select 'PDF Print' for professional business cards. Canva automatically sets them up with bleed marks, preparing them for printers.
- **Select the Color Profile:**
    - If You Have Canva Pro: Select the 'CMYK' color profile for professional printing. This ensures that the colors appear accurately in print.
    - If You Don't Have Canva Pro: Don't worry! Choose RGB, the default color profile. Your design will still look great, though there may be slight color differences in print.
- **Check File Settings:** If you use a professional printing service for banners and business cards, check the box that says "Crop marks and bleed." This helps the printer know where to trim the edges.
- **Click Download:** Once you've selected the correct file type, click Download to save your designs to your computer or USB.

PRO TIP

When saving your design files from Canva, make sure to name them clearly and organize them into folders. For example, "Pop-Up Banner_Final.pdf" or "Business Cards_Final.pdf." This way, when it's time to print, you'll easily find the correct files without digging through your downloads.

GROWTH WORK
POP UP SHOP PREP

Printing Your Sales Materials

Now that you have your files, it's time to get them printed. Here are a few options for how to print your materials:

Printing Professional Service

- **Canva.com and Vistaprint.com:** These sites are great for banners, cards, and pricing sheets. Upload your designs, choose your paper quality, and they'll deliver everything to your door.
- **FedEx Office or Staples:**
  - **Option 1:** Upload your files online and select banner and business card printing options. You can choose to pick up your prints in-store or have them delivered.
  - **Option 2**: Bring your files on a USB or email them directly to the shop. They can assist with special materials, finishes, or custom sizes.
- **Timing Matters – Make Sure to Order in Time:** To avoid last-minute stress, give yourself plenty of time to print everything before your pop-up.
  - Design your materials at least 2 weeks before your pop-up to give yourself time for revisions or any adjustments.
  - Place your order at least 1 week before your event to ensure you receive everything on time.

Printing at Home

If you can access a high-quality printer at home, you can print your business cards and pricing sheets yourself. Here's what to do:

- **Use High-Quality Paper:**
  - For business cards, use thick cardstock (about 80lb or higher).
  - For pricing sheets, regular printer paper works, but the thicker paper makes it feel more professional.
- **Set Your Printer Settings:**
  - Choose High-Quality or Best Quality in your printer settings.
  - For business cards, select the option to print with bleed (if available) to make sure the cards are cut correctly.
- **Cutting Business Cards:** Using a paper cutter or scissors to cut along the trim lines carefully after printing. Make sure the edges are clean and straight for a professional look.

GROWTH WORK
POP UP SHOP PREP

Your Check List

Whether you're offering products or services, being prepared with the right essentials will make the day go smoothly. Before your big day, take a moment to go through this list and check off these key items:

Branding and Presentation:
- [ ] Stand-up banner for visibility
- [ ] Tablecloths or backdrop for a professional look
- [ ] Product displays (for products) or service demos (for services)
- [ ] Signage with prices, promotions, or discounts
- [ ] Business cards and flyers to promote your brand

Sales and Transaction Tools:
- [ ] POS system (like Square) for credit/debit card payments
- [ ] Cash box and enough change for cash transactions
- [ ] Mobile payment apps set up for convenience

Inventory and Supplies (Product-Based Pop-Ups Only):
- [ ] Sufficient product stock based on your estimates
- [ ] Bags and packaging for customers' purchases
- [ ] Backup inventory to restock quickly if needed

Customer Engagement Materials:
- [ ] Email sign-up sheet for future promotions (bring plenty of pens)
- [ ] Giveaways or free samples to create excitement
- [ ] Interactive elements like a discount wheel or Instagram challenges

Logistics and Comfort:
- [ ] Portable tables and chairs for your setup
- [ ] Snacks and water to stay energized
- [ ] Weather protection (tent or canopy) for outdoor setups

Extras and Backups:
- [ ] Phone charger and power strips
- [ ] Cleaning supplies (wipes, sanitizer) to keep things tidy

GROWTH WORK
POST POP UP ASSESSMENT

After Your Pop Up

How did your sales go?

Total Sales: $ _____

Total Spent: $ _____

Total Profit: $ _____

Did you meet your sales goals?

☐ Yes
☐ No
☐ Exceeded It

What Worked Well?

_____

What Didn't Work?

_____

What changes will you make to improve your pop-up shop?

_____

EXCERPT FROM TEEN MAGAZINE SUMMER 2024 EDITION

Introducing Binta Camara, Make-up Artist

By Dathonie Pinto

Binta Camara, a dynamic 17-year-old entrepreneur, epitomizes the power of passion and persistence in pursuit of her dreams. Engaged in a transformative 10-week entrepreneurship program, Binta's journey began a year ago when she delved into the world of makeup artistry, honing her skills with her sister and mother. Initially, her enthusiasm outpaced her efficiency, as she found herself overspending on products. However, the program's guidance enlightened her on cost-effective procurement, empowering her to optimize her resources.

Driven by a desire to bolster her confidence and uplift others, Binta embarked on her entrepreneurial venture, propelled by her mother's unwavering encouragement to see things through. With determination as her compass, she navigated the transition from novice to professional, seizing every opportunity to showcase her talents. From humble beginnings, she launched her business, leveraging word of mouth, social media, and personal connections to cultivate her clientele.

In Binta's words, "Makeup isn't just about appearance; it's about self-expression and empowerment. It's the canvas upon which one's inner beauty is revealed to the world." As she refines her craft, her vision extends beyond mere aesthetics, aiming to craft experiences that transcend physical transformation. With her forthcoming website and captivating before-and-after shots, Binta invites others to embark on a journey of self-discovery and confidence. Watch out for Binta Camara, the creative force behind transformative beauty, ready to make you look and feel as radiant as you truly are.

YOU DID IT!

You grasped the ins and outs of marketing, using both old-school and digital tactics to promote your brand, connect with your audience across platforms, and ultimately attract buyers and drive sales. From social media to influencers to ads, you have a whole playbook now.

Content creation skills allowed you to create compelling videos, photos, blogs, and more to engage your audience, showcase your expertise, and build a loyal community around your brand.

You learned innovative strategies for product sourcing to acquire inventory or supplies and diligent budgeting to price products profitably while managing all your expenses.

Establishing your brand's presence through a professional website and social channels became a priority. You're set to create an online home for your business and leverage digital platforms to maximize your brand reach.

Mastering customer service, communication, and business etiquette will allow you to resolve issues professionally, cultivate positive relationships with your clients and contacts, and generally conduct yourself with poise in the business world.

YOU DID IT!

When it came to your pop-up shop, you learned how to create an engaging, visually appealing setup that attracts customers and showcases your products or services in the best possible light. From planning inventory and organizing your space to offering an unforgettable customer experience, you mastered every step of executing a successful pop-up event.

The knowledge and skills you've gained through this guide have provided an outstanding foundation for entrepreneurial success. But this is just the start of your journey! As you take your first steps into the business world as a teen entrepreneur, stay determined and keep adapting what you've learned here. Never stop developing yourself further through hands-on experience, additional education, and constantly seeking out new ways to grow and elevate your entrepreneurial ventures.

Your youthful entrepreneurial spirit, creativity, and drive will allow you to carve an extraordinary path. Use the tools you've acquired to turn your biggest dreams into reality. The world can't wait to see what innovative, game-changing concepts you'll introduce as the business leaders of the future!

Proud Teen Entrepreneurs and Magazine Editors stand proud in front of their Youth Voices Unheard Magazine Editions with Artist Lil' Mama and Program Director Dr. Jamila T. Davis

YOU DID IT!

As you come to the close of this book, take a moment to look back on everything you've learned about becoming a young entrepreneur. From the very start, you were inspired by the real stories of teen business owners like Trey Brown and Zandra Cunningham. Their successes at such a young age show that with passion, hard work, and a willingness to learn, you can achieve amazing things as an entrepreneurial teen.

You discovered how important it is to get smart about money—budgeting, saving, banking, investing, and building wealth over time. Understanding finances thoroughly will help you avoid debt and build a solid foundation for your future business ventures.

You learned how to take the things you really care about and turn them into viable business ideas through market research and planning. Whether it's fashion, food, tech, entertainment, or something else you love, there are ways to monetize your passions.

Branding became your creative outlet as you learned to craft an identity, story, and visuals that represent your unique brand personality and resonate with your target customers. Having a distinct, appealing brand presence is everything.

Bronx Teen Entrepreneurs receive citations from Borough President Vanessa L. Gibson and Councilman Kevin Riley. Students pictured alongside Dr. Jamila T. Davis, Principal Zenobia White, and Superintendent Fia Davis.

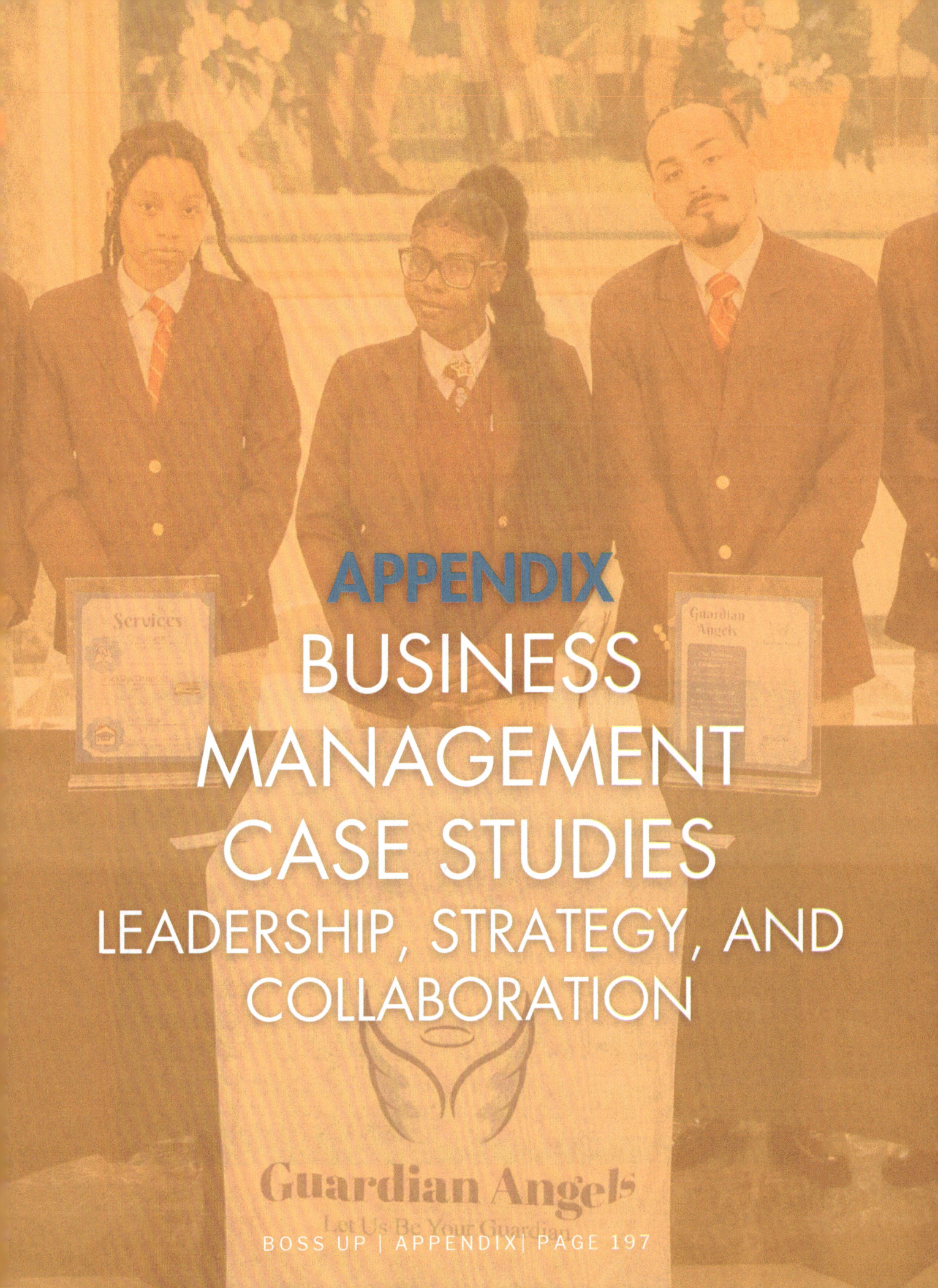

APPENDIX
BUSINESS MANAGEMENT CASE STUDIES
LEADERSHIP, STRATEGY, AND COLLABORATION

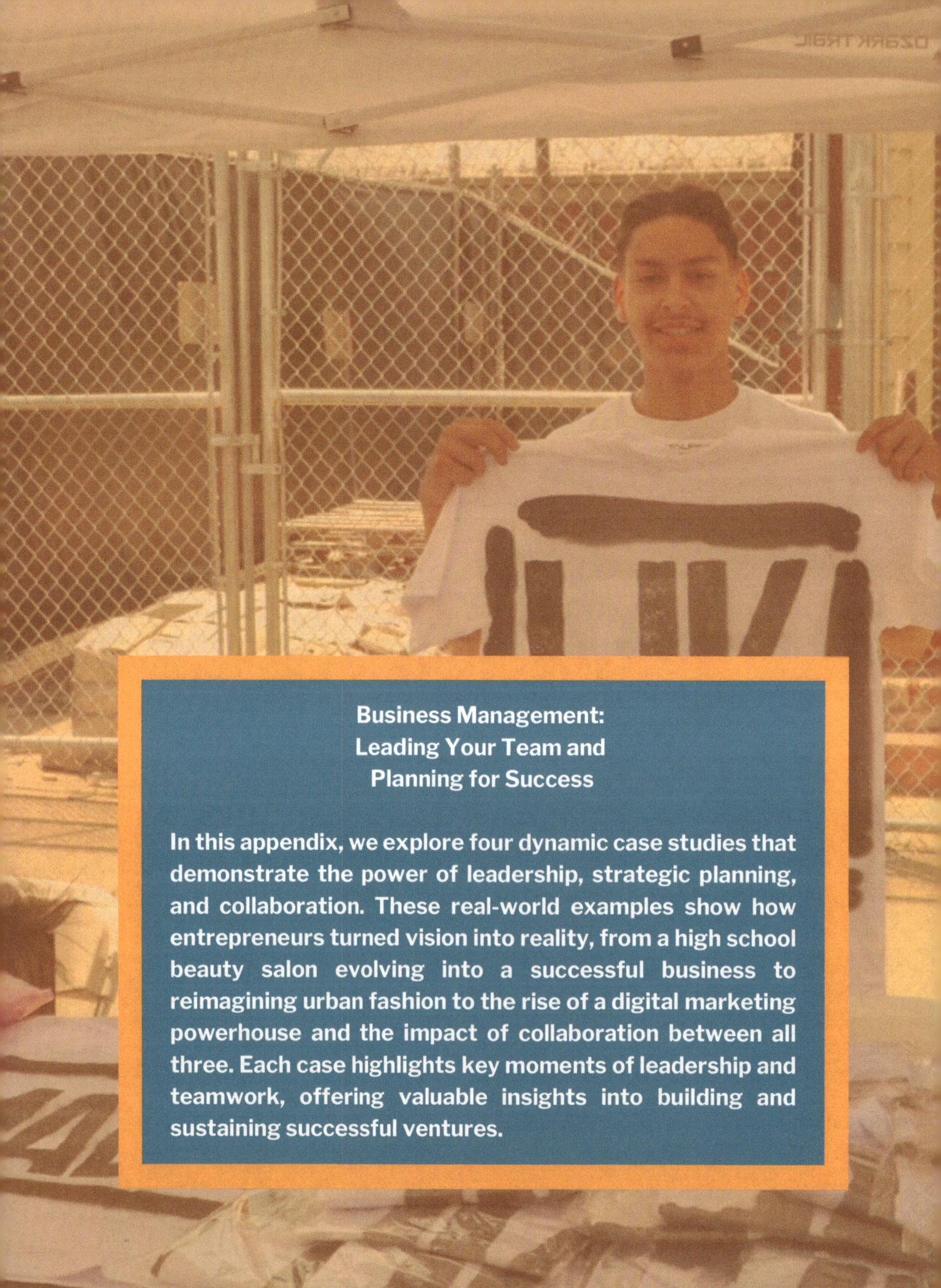

Business Management: Leading Your Team and Planning for Success

In this appendix, we explore four dynamic case studies that demonstrate the power of leadership, strategic planning, and collaboration. These real-world examples show how entrepreneurs turned vision into reality, from a high school beauty salon evolving into a successful business to reimagining urban fashion to the rise of a digital marketing powerhouse and the impact of collaboration between all three. Each case highlights key moments of leadership and teamwork, offering valuable insights into building and sustaining successful ventures.

CASE STUDIES
COLLABORATION AND LEADERSHIP

The same creativity, planning, and leadership that make a pop-up shop successful are key to elevating any business. In the following appendix, we'll explore four case studies showing how entrepreneurs in various industries used these principles to grow their ventures. These examples provide practical insights into leadership and teamwork that can help you take your business to the next level.

From Passion to Profit: How Simplicity and Teamwork Built a High School Beauty Empire dives into the story of Tracy, Cheryl, and Fran, who launched their beauty business while still in high school. Focusing on their core services and leveraging each other's strengths, they turned their passion for beauty into a successful salon serving their community.

In From Basement Startup to Showcase Success: In Malik's Journey with Urban Trendz, we follow Malik's rise in urban fashion. Starting from his mom's basement, Malik overcame financial hurdles. He built a standout brand by making strategic decisions and staying true to his vision, proving that resilience and resourcefulness are key to success.

Leverage Your Strengths, Build Your Team: Jordan's Digital Dreamers Story highlights the journey of a young entrepreneur who transformed his love for digital marketing and photography into a flourishing business. With a clear plan and a strong team, Jordan showed that knowing your strengths—and bringing in the proper support—can take a business to the next level.

Strength in Synergy: How Collaboration Drove Success for Urban Trendz, Leading Beauty, and Digital Dreamers explores how these three businesses collaborated to create partnerships that elevated each of them. Through co-branded events, creative collaborations, and joint marketing efforts, they proved that the right partnerships can amplify impact and open doors to new opportunities.

As you read these case studies, you'll see the essential role of leadership, teamwork, and collaboration in every entrepreneur's journey. Whether you're building your own business or looking for ways to grow, these stories offer valuable insights on turning passion into profit, overcoming challenges, and working together to achieve lasting success.

CASE STUDY

From Passion to Profit: How Simplicity and Teamwork Built a High School Beauty Empire

Starting a beauty salon venture as high school students might sound daunting, but it was an opportunity for Tracy, Cheryl, and Fran to turn their passion into a thriving business.

Specializing in braids, weaves, lash extensions, and nail treatments, they aimed to create a beauty haven offering top-notch services while navigating the challenges of limited resources. They called their business Leading Beauty.

Here's how Tracy, Cheryl, and Fran demonstrated exceptional leadership in turning their startup dream into a reality.

Keep it simple: Tracy, Cheryl, and Fran knew simplicity was crucial to their startup approach. They focused on mastering a select range of beauty services. Tracy nailed braids and weaves, Cheryl rocked lash extensions, and Fran slayed nail treatments. By honing their skills in these core services, they ensured their salon delivered exceptional quality, laying a solid foundation for future growth.

Use tech to your advantage: Despite being high school students, Tracy, Cheryl, and Fran were tech-savvy entrepreneurs. They understood the power of online platforms in streamlining business operations and enhancing customer experience. Together, they invested in Wix, a comprehensive website builder offering features like Wix Bookings for seamless appointment scheduling. With Wix, they effortlessly managed their salon's online presence, showcased their services, and allowed clients to book appointments conveniently from any device.

Stick to the plan: Tracy, Cheryl, and Fran developed a clear business plan outlining their goals and strategies for success. They identified their target market, mapped out their service offerings, and set achievable milestones to track their progress. Despite facing challenges like limited funds and time constraints, they remained committed to their vision and diligently followed their plan, guiding them toward success.

From Passion to Profit: How Simplicity and Teamwork Built a High School Beauty Empire

Trust your network: Recognizing the power of collaboration, Tracy, Cheryl, and Fran formed a strong partnership to support each other's businesses. They pooled their resources to secure a space at a salon suite through Fran's aunt, sharing the cost of rent and associated fees. Additionally, they each covered their own supplies expenses, ensuring independence while maximizing cost efficiency. This network of mutual support expanded their customer base and maximized their earning potential.

Learn as you go: Like any startup journey, Tracy, Cheryl, and Fran embraced continuous learning and adaptation. They welcomed feedback from each other and their clients, seeking opportunities to enhance their skills and services. Whether mastering new braiding techniques, staying updated on nail trends, or refining their online presence with Wix, they were always eager to evolve and improve as beauty professionals.

Leading Beauty's Conclusion:

Tracy, Cheryl, and Fran's leadership glittered at every turn of their entrepreneurial journey. From the simplicity of their business model to their savvy use of technology, they demonstrated that staying focused on core strengths can yield significant rewards. Their ability to trust in their network, lean on one another's expertise, and embrace continuous learning allowed them to overcome obstacles and turn their dream into reality.

By remaining committed to their plan, they built a profitable business and a strong foundation for future growth. Leading Beauty stands as a testament to visionary leadership, where collaboration, resilience, and smart decision-making drive success. Their story serves as an inspiration to aspiring entrepreneurs, showcasing the immense power of effective leadership, teamwork, and shared goals in building something truly remarkable.

CASE STUDY

From Basement Startup to Showcase Success: Malik's Journey with Urban Trendz

In the bustling world of urban fashion, Malik embarked on a journey fueled by passion and perseverance. Starting Urban Trendz from his mom's basement, Malik faced numerous challenges as he strived to realize his vision.

This case study follows Malik's remarkable journey, highlighting his strategic decisions, financial hurdles, and ultimate triumphs as Urban Trendz evolves from a humble startup to a standout success.

Here's how Malik demonstrated his leadership during start-up mode:

Seize Opportunities: As Urban Trendz gained traction in the urban fashion scene, Malik encountered a pivotal opportunity: a showcase event that promised exposure and potential partnerships. However, participation in the showcase required a significant financial investment, presenting a challenge for Malik. With limited resources and a tight budget, Malik faced the daunting task of securing funding to seize this valuable opportunity for Urban Trendz.

Cultivate Belief and Support: Undeterred by the financial constraints, Malik sought support from an individual who shared his belief in Urban Trendz's potential. This supportive figure recognized Malik's vision and commitment and offered financial assistance to help Urban Trendz participate in the showcase. With this crucial funding secured, Malik was able to cover the costs associated with the showcase, including booth fees, promotional materials, and travel expenses.

Build a Talented Team: To ensure Urban Trendz's success at the showcase, Malik made the strategic decision to hire two contractors: Lisa, a skilled marketer, and Tom, a talented graphic designer. Despite their limited budget, through careful negotiations and a shared passion for the brand's vision, Malik enlisted Lisa and Tom to contribute their expertise to Urban Trendz's showcase preparations.

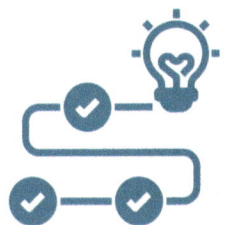

From Basement Startup to Showcase Success: Malik's Journey with Urban Trendz

Prioritize Transparency and Integrity: Recognizing the importance of financial transparency and accountability, Malik established a clear agreement with Lisa and Tom regarding their compensation. Despite the initial financial strain, Malik committed to repaying the borrowed funds by a specified date, ensuring Lisa and Tom would receive fair compensation for their valuable contributions to Urban Trendz's success. This mutual understanding and commitment to financial integrity underscored Malik's dedication to his team and his business's long-term sustainability.

Navigating Challenges: With the support of his team and the financial backing of his investor, Malik navigated the challenges of the showcase with confidence and determination. Urban Trendz's booth attracted attention and admiration, introducing its unique designs and urban aesthetic to a diverse audience of industry professionals and potential customers. The event proved to be a turning point for Urban Trendz, solidifying its reputation and opening doors to new opportunities for growth and expansion.

Malik's Conclusion:

Malik's journey with Urban Trendz exemplifies the resilience, resourcefulness, and entrepreneurial spirit required to succeed in the competitive world of fashion entrepreneurship. Through strategic decision-making, financial prudence, and a steadfast commitment to his vision, Malik transformed Urban Trendz from a basement startup into a showcase success story.

By overcoming financial hurdles, building a talented team, and seizing opportunities for growth, Malik demonstrated the power of passion and perseverance in achieving entrepreneurial dreams. As Urban Trendz continues to thrive and evolve, Malik's journey serves as an inspiration to aspiring entrepreneurs everywhere, proving that with dedication and determination, anything is possible in the world of business.

CASE STUDY

Leverage Your Strengths, Build Your Team: Jordan's Digital Dreamers Story

Meet Jordan, a high school student with a big dream: to create a digital marketing and photography company called Digital Dreamers. Jordan is determined to make his mark in the world of entrepreneurship.

This case study follows Jordan's journey as he turns his passion for digital marketing and photography into a thriving business:

Know Where You're Going: When Jordan came up with Digital Dreamers, he had a clear picture in his mind. He wanted it to be the go-to spot for digital marketing and photography services in his city. His goal was simple: help local businesses get noticed online and reel in more customers. With that vision burning bright, Jordan dove into the entrepreneurial game, ready to rock and roll.

Set Goals: Jordan wasn't just winging it; he had a plan. He set specific goals to keep himself on track. He aimed to snag ten clients in the first six months, rake in $5,000 in revenue by the end of the year, and expand into social media management within a year. These goals weren't just dreams; they were his roadmap to success.

Know Your Strengths and Weaknesses: Jordan knew his strengths—creativity and people skills—but he also knew where he needed backup. That's where his cousin Leah and his buddy Sean came in. His cousin Leah was a social media queen, and his buddy Sean was a wizard with websites and graphics.

By teaming up, they covered each other's backs and made Digital Dreamers a force to be reckoned with, each bringing something unique to the table. Jordan even sweetened the deal by offering Leah and Sean a 10% cut for every new client they brought in. Talk about motivation!

Leverage Your Strengths, Build Your Team: Jordan's Digital Dreamers Story

Make a Plan: With his dream team in place, Jordan got down to business, mapping out a solid plan for Digital Dreamers. He outlined strategies for snagging clients, managing projects, and expanding their services—all while keeping an eye on the bottom line. Every dollar was carefully allocated to marketing, equipment, and other essentials, making sure they stayed within budget while raking in the profits.

Keep an Eye on the Prize: Through all the ups and downs, Jordan never lost sight of the finish line. He kept his eyes on the prize, pushing through obstacles and setbacks like a boss. His determination and focus turned Digital Dreamers from a dream into a reality, proving that with the right mindset, anything is possible.

Jordan's Conclusion:

Jordan's journey with Digital Dreamers highlights the creativity, strategic thinking, and leadership it takes to succeed in the world of digital marketing and photography. By setting clear goals, building a strong team, and staying focused on his vision, Jordan transformed Digital Dreamers from an idea into a thriving business.

Through leveraging his strengths, empowering his team, and pushing through challenges, Jordan demonstrated the power of collaboration and determination in turning a dream into reality. As Digital Dreamers continues to grow, Jordan's story stands as an example to aspiring young entrepreneurs everywhere, proving that with focus and teamwork, anything is possible in business.

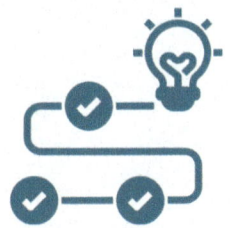

LEADERSHIP CASE STUDIES SUMMARY

Leading Your Team: Bringing Out the Best in Others

These three case studies demonstrate that entrepreneurial success isn't just about your talents. You also have to harness the power of your team. Building a rockstar crew that shares your vision and brings out the best in each other is key. Here's how the pros energize the people they lead to reach new heights together.

Lead by Example: Malik from Urban Trendz doesn't just talk the talk; he lives and breathes his brand. From sketching new designs to packing orders, he's hands-on in every facet. Malik's unstoppable hustle sets the pace, inspiring his squad to match that same grit and attention to detail. When your team sees you putting in the work, they'll go all in, too.

Open Dialogue: At Leading Beauty, the trio of Tracy, Cheryl, and Fran share leadership and prioritize open communication. They huddle up weekly to sync on upcoming bookings, troubleshoot any speed bumps, and riff on ideas for improving their services. By nurturing that safe space for real talk, they empower their team to freely contribute thoughts and solutions.

Spread Positive Energy: Jordan at Digital Dreamers knows the power of a pumped-up vibe. He champions a supportive, high-energy culture that brings out the best in everyone. Whether it's shouting out team wins or dropping kudos bombs, Jordan's enthusiasm is contagious, boosting morale and inspiring peak performance.

Invest in Growth: The Leading Beauty ladies never stop leveling up their skills. They're constantly seeking training on the latest techniques, ensuring their team remains ahead of the curve. By nurturing continuous learning and development, they unlock new talents and empower their crew to elevate their artistry.

Give Props: At Urban Trendz, Malik showers his team with props when they knock it out of the park. Smashing sales goals? Expect a shout-out on the company's social channels and website and sweet bonuses. Recognizing stellar work doesn't just make your team feel valued—it stokes their motivation to keep improving.

CASE STUDIES

Strength in Synergy: How Collaboration Drove Success for Urban Trendz, Leading Beauty, and Digital Dreamers

In the dynamic landscape of entrepreneurship, **collaboration** often leads to innovative solutions and mutual growth. Urban Trendz, Leading Beauty, and Digital Dreamers represent three distinct ventures that have made significant strides in their respective industries. This case study explores how these diverse businesses come together to leverage their strengths, complement each other's offerings, and create synergies that benefit both their individual enterprises and the wider entrepreneurial community.

Each of these companies can be viewed as potential **partners** rather than competitors. Each company operates in a different niche within the beauty and digital marketing industries, offering unique products or services. By collaborating, they can leverage each other's strengths, expand their offerings, and reach new markets.

For example, Urban Trendz offers trendy clothing and accessories, Leading Beauty specializes in beauty services, and Digital Dreamers provides digital marketing and photography services. Together, they can create synergies that benefit all parties involved and enhance their overall competitiveness in their respective markets.

Collaborative Initiatives:
Despite operating in different sectors, Urban Trendz, Leading Beauty, and Digital Dreamers recognize the value of collaboration and have initiated several joint ventures to capitalize on their collective strengths.

Cross-Promotional Campaigns:
By partnering on marketing initiatives, such as social media campaigns and influencer collaborations, the three ventures amplify their reach and exposure, tapping into each other's customer bases and fostering brand loyalty across diverse audiences.

Co-Branded Events:
Urban Trendz hosts fashion pop-ups featuring hair and beauty services by Leading Beauty, with Digital Dreamers providing event coverage and digital marketing support. These collaborative events not only drive foot traffic and sales but also create immersive brand experiences for customers.

Strength in Synergy: How Collaboration Drove Success for Urban Trendz, Leading Beauty, and Digital Dreamers

Creative Collaborations:
Urban Trendz collaborates with Digital Dreamers on photo shoots and promotional videos, showcasing Urban Trendz apparel in visually captivating digital content produced by Digital Dreamers. Leading Beauty provides hair and makeup services for these collaborations, adding an extra layer of creativity and expertise.

Mentorship Programs:
Digital Dreamers offers mentorship programs for aspiring entrepreneurs in collaboration with Urban Trendz and Leading Beauty. Through workshops, seminars, and one-on-one coaching sessions, seasoned entrepreneurs share their insights and expertise, empowering the next generation of business leaders.

The Collab Conclusion:
The collaboration between Urban Trendz, Leading Beauty, and Digital Dreamers highlights how synergy can drive innovation, expand reach, and create new business opportunities. By joining forces through cross-promotional campaigns, co-branded events, and creative partnerships, these businesses leveraged each other's strengths to grow beyond their individual capabilities.

Their collective efforts show that collaboration is a vital tool for long-term success in an ever-changing business landscape. From mentorship programs to joint ventures, they've proven that working together not only enhances their individual growth but also inspires others to embrace teamwork as a path to shared success.

COLLABORATION CASE STUDY SUMMARY

The collaboration case study showed that entrepreneurship thrives on more than individual effort—it's about how you work with others to create something bigger. Collaboration isn't just about working together; it's about combining strengths to unlock new opportunities and grow in ways you couldn't do alone.

Here are the steps successful entrepreneurs take to leverage partnerships, amplify their impact, and elevate their businesses to the next level.

Step 1: Reflect on Your Business Goals
Take a moment to reflect on your business goals and aspirations. Consider what you hope to achieve with your venture and any challenges you may face in reaching those goals.

Step 2: Identify Potential Collaborators
Think about other businesses or entrepreneurs in your industry who could complement your offerings or provide valuable resources. Research their businesses and values to determine if they align with your goals and values.

Step 3: Brainstorm Collaboration Ideas
Brainstorm potential collaboration ideas that could benefit both your business and your potential partners. Consider how you could leverage each other's strengths, resources, and networks to create value for your customers and drive mutual growth.

Step 4: Evaluate Collaboration Potential
Evaluate each collaboration idea based on its potential impact, feasibility, and alignment with your business goals:

- **Impact:** Assess the potential benefits of the collaboration for your business, such as increased visibility, access to new markets, or expanded product offerings.
- **Feasibility:** Consider the practicality of implementing each collaboration idea, taking into account factors like resource requirements, timeline, and potential challenges.
- **Alignment with Business Goals**: Evaluate how well each collaboration idea aligns with your long-term business objectives and strategic priorities.

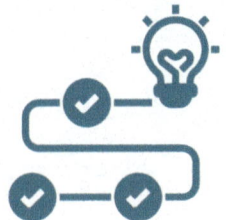

Collaboration Case Study Summary

Step 5: Develop A Collaboration Plan
Choose one or more collaboration ideas to pursue and develop a detailed plan for implementing your ideas.

- **Roles and Responsibilities:** Define the roles and responsibilities of each partner involved in the collaboration, outlining who will be responsible for what tasks and deliverables.
- **Timelines and Milestones:** Establish timelines and milestones for the collaboration, setting clear deadlines for critical activities and deliverables.
- **Key Metrics for Success:** Identify key metrics for measuring the collaboration's success, such as increased sales, customer satisfaction, or brand visibility.

Step 6: Implementation and Review
Implement your collaboration plan and monitor its progress over time. Regularly review the collaboration to assess its effectiveness and make any necessary adjustments to ensure its success. Celebrate milestones and achievements along the way, and continue to nurture your partnerships for long-term growth and success.

Collab Conclusion:

Collaborative ventures can accelerate growth, drive innovation, and create value for all parties involved. By embracing collaboration as a strategic tool in your entrepreneurial journey, you can unlock new opportunities, overcome challenges, and achieve greater success than you ever thought possible.

So, take the first step today and explore potential collaborators who can help you realize your business dreams.

GLOSSARY

Assets:
Things you own that are worth money, like a cool bike, your savings in the bank, or a collection of rare cards. They're things that can help you get more money in the future.

Affiliate marketing:
This is when you team up with another company or business to help them sell their stuff, and you get a cut of the money when someone buys through your link or promotion.

Algorithm:
This is a set of rules that a computer follows. Social media apps like TikTok, Instagram, and YouTube use algorithms to decide what videos and posts to show you.

Analytics:
This is like being a detective for your business. You look at data to understand what people like and how your business is doing online. It helps you figure out how to improve your business and what is working well.

Authenticity:
Being real and true to yourself, and making sure your brand also feels real and true.
Branding: Giving your business its own personality. It's how people recognize you and what makes your business different. It includes:
- Your Logo: The special picture or symbol that represents your business.
- Your Colors: The specific colors you use to make your business stand out.
- Your Story: What makes your business special and why you do what you do.
- How you treat customers: What you say when someone buys something and how you respond if they have a problem.
- Personal Branding: Creating your own special identity, telling people what you are good at, what you like, and what makes you, you.
- Brand Guide: A rulebook for your business that makes sure everything looks the same, so everyone recognizes your brand. This includes the logo, colors, and fonts (the style of your letters).
- Tagline: This is a catchy phrase that summarizes what your brand is all about.

Business Etiquette:
The way you act professionally in business situations, showing respect and good manners to customers, partners, and others

GLOSSARY

Business Plan:
A map for your business. It shows where you want to go and how you plan to get there. It includes:
- Executive Summary: A short summary of your entire plan, like the highlights of your map. It tells people what your business is about, who you want to sell to, and how you'll make money.
- Mission Statement: Like your business's purpose, what it wants to do for its customers and the community.
- Vision Statement: What your business hopes to be in the future, like a dream for your business, what you want to accomplish in the long term.

Bylaws:
These are the rules for how a corporation is run. It's like an instruction manual for your business.

Collaboration:
When you work with other people or businesses that do something similar to you. This can help you reach more people, make new friends, and share cool ideas.
Competitive Analysis: Looking at other businesses like yours to see what they do well, what they don't do so well, and how you can be different and better. It's like studying your competitors to win.

Content Creation:
Making cool stuff to share with people, like videos, blog posts, or pictures. It's how you show people what your business is about and get them interested in what you're doing.
- User Generated Content (UGC): Content that other people make about your business. You can share their posts to show that they like your brand and how other customers are using your products.

Corporation:
A type of business that is like its own separate person, it has its own legal identity and is separate from the people who own it.

Cost of Goods Sold (COGS):
How much money it costs you to make or buy the stuff you sell.

Credit:
Borrowing money or buying something and paying for it later. If you use it wisely, it can help you buy things that you can use to make more money.

Customer Service:
How you help people who buy from your business. Being helpful, polite, and quick to respond makes people like your business more.

GLOSSARY

Digital Marketing:
Using the internet to market your business.

Disclaimers:
These are statements that say you're not responsible if something goes wrong with the information on your website. It's like a "just in case" warning.

Diversify:
To add a variety of different things, like products or services, to your business.

Financial Literacy:
Knowing how to manage your money. It includes understanding how to save, budget, and spend wisely.

Generational Wealth:
When families pass down their wealth from parents to children and so on.
Grossing: This is the total amount of money you make before taking out any costs.

Intellectual Property:
This is the legal right that says that creative content (like images and text) belongs to the person who made it. People need your permission to use your work, which you own.
Liabilities: Your debts or bills that you need to pay. It's a good idea to try to keep these as low as possible.

Limited Liability Company (LLC):
A type of business that protects the owners from being personally responsible for the company's debts, it combines some of the benefits of a partnership and a corporation.

Logistics:
This is how you plan and manage getting your products or services to your customers. It's all about making sure your stuff gets to the right place at the right time.

Marketing:
How you tell people about your business and get them to buy your products or services.

Monetization:
Turning your content or business into money-making opportunities. It's when you get paid for the content you create or services you provide.

GLOSSARY

Niche:
A specific area or focus for your business, where you have special skills or knowledge.

Operational costs:
The costs associated with running your business everyday, such as equipment and utilities.

Partnership:
When two or more people agree to own and run a business together.

Passive Income:
Money you earn without actively working all the time. For instance, if you sell things online, you might earn money even when you're sleeping.

Pop-Up Shop:
A temporary store you set up to show off your business, sell your products, and meet customers in person.

Pricing:
How much money you charge for the things you sell. You have to make sure the price is right so you can pay for your stuff and also make some money.

Profit:
The money you make after you pay all your costs. Think of it as the "Big Flip" - the extra money that comes back to you after spending some to get started.

Reinvesting:
Taking the money you make and putting it back into your business to help it grow. It's like planting seeds to grow more trees.

Responsive design:
Making sure your website looks good on any device, like phones and tablets.

Return on Investment (ROI):
Measuring if your marketing investments were worth it, and if you are making a profit from the money you spend.

Revenue:
The total amount of money your business brings in from sales, before you take away your costs.

GLOSSARY

Responsive design:
Making sure your website looks good on any device, like phones and tablets.

Return on Investment (ROI):
Measuring if your marketing investments were worth it, and if you are making a profit from the money you spend.

Revenue:
The total amount of money your business brings in from sales, before you take away your costs.

S.M.A.R.T. Goals:
A way to make your goals easier to achieve. This means your goals should be:
- Specific: Know exactly what you want to do.
- Measurable: Be able to track your progress.
- Achievable: Set goals that you have a good chance of reaching.
- Relevant: Make sure the goals are useful for your business.
- Time-bound: Give your goals a deadline.

Shareholder:
Someone who owns a part of a corporation. They own stocks that show how much of the corporation that they own.

Social Entrepreneur:
Someone who starts a business that also helps the community and makes the world a better place.

Sole Proprietorship:
A business owned and run by just one person.

Sponsored content:
Content that you create in partnership with a brand where they pay you to showcase their products or services. It's like a commercial, but it is made by you, to showcase a brand you use or believe in.

Tagline:
This is a catchy phrase that summarizes what your brand is all about.

Target audience:
The specific group of people you want to sell your product or service to, they share traits such as age, gender, and interests.

GLOSSARY

Terms of Use:
These are the rules that people have to follow to use your website. It's like an agreement they make with you when they use your site.

Value proposition:
What makes your business special and why customers should choose you instead of your competitors.

Wholesalers:
Businesses that sell things in large amounts to other businesses, usually at a lower price.

NOTES

NOTES

NOTES

NOTES

NOTES

NOTES

NOTES

NOTES

FOR MORE INFORMATION ABOUT THE BOSS UP PROGRAM PLEASE VISIT VOICESBOOKS.COM/BOSSUP

Made in the USA
Coppell, TX
20 February 2026